"Every morning of their dusty journey, ground: *manna*. That was the mysterious them, kept them on the way. Pastor's boo.. ... . your soul. The mysteries within cannot be fully understood, or even articulated, but they will feed you. I commend this book heartily. Get up. Your morning has come. Eat the mystery that this book describes."

> **–Dr. A.J. Swoboda**, author of *The Dusty Ones: Why Wandering Deepens Your Faith* and pastor of Theophilus Church in Portland, Oregon

"With the debut of *The Listening Day*, I can say with great confidence and enthusiasm that Paul J. Pastor is one of the best spiritual writers of this generation. In fact, this breathtakingly beautiful offering has turned Pastor into one of my favorite writers of all time. It is clear that each meditation is the fruit of unhurried time spent in the presence of God. As you read, you will be nourished with the nourishment Pastor received from God. It has truly been a means of grace to me–a great gift. I will recommend it to everyone I know."

> **–Marlena Graves**, author of *A Beautiful Disaster: Finding Hope in the Midst of Brokenness*

"The lofty work of considering the divine can often be disembodied and disconnected from earthbound beauty and the human condition. Paul reattaches the divine and the human in a poetic and thoughtful reading experience."

> **–Dan Haseltine**, founder of Blood:Water and lead singer of Jars of Clay

"My heart's desire is to trust; to live inside the grace of one day. In your hands is a brilliantly crafted companion for your journey into living that grace. I love *The Listening Day* because it is helping me do just that."

> **–Wm Paul Young**, author of *The Shack, Cross Roads, Eve: A Novel*, and *Lies We Believe about God*

"*The Listening Day* is a devotional of creative exercise for the way we interact with both our own hearts and with God. At turns surprising, poignant, joyful, and devastating, Pastor invites us into new ways of seeing on each page. It caused me to notice both the rocky and the soft soil in the garden of my heart, and by the end, I had already discovered new places where the truly good news was able to bloom."

–**D.L. Mayfield,** author of *Assimilate or Go Home: Notes from a Failed Missionary on Rediscovering Faith*

"Here is a book to be read slowly and savored. These meditations will help you become more present to God and more aware of his work in your life and the world. Read and be nourished."

–**Dr. Krish Kandiah**, author of *Paradoxology: Why Christianity Was Never Meant to Be Simple* and founding director of Home for Good

"God speaks in these pages. As someone who has sat weeping in the church parking lot because of personal tragedy, I'm telling you: God will speak to you here. If God has been silent, if God seems far off, or cruel, then come rediscover the surprising depths of his kindness and love in this book."

–**Matt Mikalatos**, author of *Sky Lantern: The Story of a Father's Love and the Healing Power of a Simple Letter*

"Our activist age is eager to expend energy doing things for God but devotes so little energy seeking to be with him. Paul Pastor's wonderful book can help you correct this imbalance. Here you'll discover a deeper, more beautiful and life-giving communion with God."

–**Skye Jethani**, author and co-host of The Phil Vischer Podcast

"I know what you're thinking. *Not another devotional!* Here's why you'll want to give *The Listening Day* a chance: The entries are beautiful. It's classic Paul Pastor—fresh, biblical insights delivered with soaring, lyrical prose. The short entries adopt the divine perspective, but never in a way that feels forced or irreverent. Readers will be comforted, inspired, confronted—all with the purpose of helping them live a more faithful, more joyful Christian life. What a perfect way to start each morning!"

—**Drew Dyck**, senior editor of CTpastors.com and author of *Yawning at Tigers: You Can't Tame God, So Stop Trying.*

"If you are looking for a new take on the timeless message of Scripture, then you will find *The Listening Day* to be a breath of fresh air. These daily devotions are pithy, poetic, and inspiring. This book will be a perfect resource for starting your day with a deeper connection to God."

—**Daniel Hill,** author of *10:10: Life to the Fullest,* and *White Awake*

"Against the cacophony of our boisterous and bombastic times, it is very difficult to find solitude and rest. All too often, we race through our days and fail to live in the present. Paul Pastor's *The Listening Day* provides metaphorical musings that stir the heart and still the mind so that we can listen to God's Word and respond in the quiet. Renewing and enlivening. Just what the spiritual doctor ordered."

—**Paul Louis Metzger, PhD**, Professor of Christian Theology and Culture, Multnomah University and author of *Evangelical Zen: A Christian's Spiritual Travels with a Buddhist Friend*

"Too much of our time with the spiritual disciplines is rushed. We look for a nugget to take away or for secret coded messages. But *The Listening Day* invites us to slow down as we pursue Jesus, to listen to the Word of God as it washes afresh over our souls. It invites us to meditate, reflect, repent, and be renewed. Pastor's poetic, creative approach will help you worship more deeply as you daily listen to the voice of God in His Word. I highly recommend *The Listening Day.*"

—**Daniel Darling**, author of *The Original Jesus: Trading the Myths We Create for the Savior Who Is*

"Seeking justice and loving mercy can get overwhelming. Paul J. Pastor's *The Listening Day* is a balm for the weary soul. Instead of presenting the reader with yet another list of concerns with which to assail God, Pastor invites the reader to encounter God in the ever-present now. I can think of nothing more important in our age than developing the capacity to slow down and re-center ourselves on God, the source of our strength. For advocates and activists alike, this is required reading."

—**R. Anderson Campbell**, co-author of *Praying for Justice: A Lectionary of Christian Concern*

"Is time spent in reflection a work God does in us? Or a work we do for him? These evocative reflections help us imagine a better reality than either: that God invites us into conversation. We take turns speaking and listening to him—and sometimes just sitting in comfortable silence together. In *The Listening Day*, less is more (the reflections are brief) but set aside all concerns about quantity. Each page is an invitation to engage the Creator."

—**Mandy Smith,** author of *The Vulnerable Pastor: How Human Limitations Empower Our Ministry* and pastor of University Christian Church in Cincinnati, Ohio

THE
LISTENING
DAY

MEDITATIONS ON THE WAY

VOLUME ONE

PAUL J. PASTOR

z | ZEALbooks

Published by Zeal Books
537 SE Ash St., Suite 203 / Portland, OR 97214 USA / www.zealbooks.com

Cover Design: Connie Gabbert, Connie Gabbert Design + Illustration
Interior Design and Typeset: Katherine Lloyd, The Desk

Library of Congress Cataloging-in-Publication Data
Names: Pastor, Paul J., author
Title: The listening day: meditations on the way volume one / Paul J. Pastor.
Description: Portland: Zeal Books, 2017
Identifiers: LCCN 2017934303 | ISBN 9780997066968 (paperback)
ISBN 9780997066975 (ebook)
Subjects: LCHS: Christian life | devotional
Classification: LC Record available at https://lccn.loc.gov/2017934303

Printed in the United States of America
First Edition 2017
17 18 19 20 21 22 BP 6 5 4 3 2 1

For
my children

CONTENTS

FROM THE PUBLISHER

You are holding a very special book in your hands.

Paul and I were working on edits for *The Listening Day* one afternoon and after reading several entries, I got up from my chair, walked over to Paul and with tears in my eyes, just hugged him. I felt his writing had ushered the divine right into my home.

This is our prayer for you—that when you read these entries, you would encounter God. As you hear Gods voice through Paul's contemplative meditations, may your soul be stirred to respond.

We offer this book to you by faith for God's glory.

Don Jacobson, *Publisher*

ⓩ | ZEALbooks

TO THE READER

God cannot be known in the past. He cannot be known in the future. To him, all times are now—and the Father invites us to join him, to know him, now. We must learn to quiet ourselves and listen for his voice every day.

The Listening Day is a collection of responses to Scripture that focus on the meaning and power of the present. As you read, you will see each entry begins with Scripture—two connected passages to meditate upon throughout your day. I hope you will concentrate on those verses as you read. Those are the perfect words, completely truthful. The bulk of the entry is a conversation between the Father and me based on those passages—what I hear him saying to me through his Word, with one or two lines of my own heart's response. I hope my replies feel as though you might have said them, too.

This book is meant to be your personal companion throughout weeks and months, or perhaps an even longer season. It shouldn't be skimmed quickly or without thought for how these truths touch your life. Instead:

- Read this book slowly—no more than one entry per day.
- Read this book prayerfully. Quiet your mind and give your time fully to the Father, for he wants to share this moment with you.
- Read this book with an open Bible and an open heart, listening to the voice of God's Spirit communicate how each thought and word can help you know him today.

You'll notice right away that this book is written poetically, with many metaphors for God and the Christian life. These figurative elements nearly all arise from similar poetic analogies in the Bible. I've chosen to repeat a few images and themes throughout this collection, just as the biblical authors returned again and again to the same metaphors to describe the indescribable. I hope these creative expressions help you imagine God's work and character in a new way—even if you're not usually comfortable with poetry. There is much meaning here to uncover, and most of it lies just below the surface.

A note on the Scriptures: One of the most important elements of responsibly reading the Bible is keeping its words in context, ensuring that we honor the intent of the people who wrote them through the Holy Spirit.

A project like this necessarily pulls verses from their context. Think of it like pulling threads from an intricate tapestry to point out their individual power, color, and intrigue—all in pursuit of better knowing and loving the whole. I have done my best in *The Listening Day* to maintain complete faithfulness to the original meaning of the verses. I highly encourage you to read the verses in their original placement.

Any good thing in this book is the Lord's. Any mistake is my own.

> May the Father bless you on this journey of life.
> May Jesus Christ the Son claim you fully as his own.
> May the Holy Spirit fill and enlighten your heart,
> and may you find all the secret riches of God abundantly
>   given to you.
> This very day.
> This very now.

Today,

if you hear his voice,

do not harden your heart.

The one who made the Pleiades and Orion,
and turns deep darkness into the morning,
and darkens the day into night,
who calls for the waters of the sea,
and pours them out on the surface of the earth,
the LORD is his name.

Amos 5:8 (NRSV)

DAWN

Sleeper, awake! Rise from the dead,
and Christ will shine on you.

Ephesians 5:14 (NRSV)

Look to the east. You hungered for the light, and now it is coming. The first rays are faint, only a sliver of the darkness that is not as dark as the rest. The sun is the Son—Christ, the hope of life, yesterday, today, forever. He shakes the earth gently at first, like one who wakes a sleeper from dreams.

Wake me, too!

I want to see you as you are, not as I have imagined you to be.

Be careful what you ask, for those who ask receive. All my ways are love, but few of them are easy. Waking angers the one who has overslept.

Watch the sun rise, rousing the beasts and birds, rousing the trees and sweetgrass, stirring up all that fly, that splash, that crawl, that burrow. The cities waken, near and far—also the pilgrims, the farmers, the guests to the wedding that will come in the evening. Up stand the soldiers, the children, the prisoners. Up stand the priests and the whores. All see the Son, though they can only squint in the light at first.

Hear! He is calling all to walk in the manner of God's own, in the quiet and the riot, the common and the holy of the listening day.

I am standing too.

Lord, you are invading the world through Jesus. Let my heart
be teachable and ready to grow in your ways and in your works,
living out the light you have begun to shine in my heart. Amen.

1

Do not boast about tomorrow,
for you do not know what a day may bring.
Proverbs 27:1 (NRSV)

WHAT A DAY MAY BRING

What is your life? For you are a mist that appears for
a little while and then vanishes. Instead you ought to say,
"If the Lord wishes, we will live and do this or that."
James 4:14–15 (NRSV)

Today could see you laugh
or weep,
curse the heavens,
or bless the whole world.
It could see you fall into the
    darkest sin
or rise to unimagined
    righteousness.
It could hold death for your
    family,
sickness for your friends,
good fortune for your enemy,
or the opposite of all those.
You could lose your reputation
    today
or gain a better one.
You could feast
or find yourself hungry.
You might be alive when the
    stars appear tonight.

You might not be.
All your plans could go through,
or none of them,
like a breeze carries the morning
    fog
to places the mist doesn't
    choose.
Boast of nothing.

Of what can I be confident, then?

Your Father's love.
Turn to me. I am faithful.
I promise: though the world is
    changeable,
carrying you where you don't
    expect,
my goodness is in every place.
I will help you find it
and learn to rest forever in my
    hand.

Father, you know my past, present, and future.
Help me to put no confidence in myself and reject boasting.
Let me expect nothing of life except to know you better
and love you fully, regardless of my circumstances. Amen.

God said, "Let there be light";
and there was light.

Genesis 1:3 (NRSV)

LET LIGHT BE

The people who walked in darkness
have seen a great light;
those who lived in a land of deep darkness—
on them light has shined.

Isaiah 9:2 (NRSV)

﮳

You do not yet understand, Child of Adam, that existence is war. Every sound you ever heard was a mighty triumph—a victory over infinite silence. Every beam of light comes to you after winning a battle for its life among the hosts of darkness.

What does that mean for me?

That you must expect nothing less.

The life of God is the roughest kind of work: a field that must be plowed, a road that leads through steep and strange places, a lover who must be wooed, a battle to win in the coming morning.

All has been done for you in Jesus, but now you must live it all out. You must fight for the kingdom that was won for you before your race drew breath.

Help me.

Yours will be the power of my Spirit, the help of my people, the sure guidance of my Word. All good and true things will call you cousin, for you will be an ally of the light. This morning will see you walking well, and by my grace this evening will find you at my table.
Let light be in you. You will overcome.

﮳

Father, you have called your people to what we could never do in our
own power: living like Christ in the midst of a cruel and difficult world.
Help me to rejoice in the challenge of life and look to you for
all power and guidance. Amen.

3

I delight in the way of your decrees
as much as in all riches.
I will meditate on your precepts,
and fix my eyes on your ways.
Psalm 119:14–15 (NRSV)

THE UNSEEN WAY

By faith we understand that the universe was formed at God's command,
so that what is seen was not made out of what was visible.
Hebrews 11:3 (NIV)

Your life is lived in the little things.
Not in decades, but in days.
Not in days, but in moments.
Not in moments, but in milliseconds.
Not in any time at all, but only in the now, which is always.
Now is where the world touches eternity.

I am so scattered and distracted. How can I know you?

In this moment, be present. Quiet yourself to hear my voice. Call your mind back from the alleys where it wanders. Be one with yourself, and be at peace.

I don't think I can.

You will learn. Eternity touches time precisely where I meet you. The great unseen kisses the world you see, and all the past and all the future fade, for our moment of knowing is now.

The way to me must be lived one now at a time. I will teach you this skill, but you need to do one thing.

What is it?

Ask me to turn today into eternity. Ask me to make this now heaven.

Lord, you are the perfectly present God. Help me gather my scattered self,
eliminating worry and distraction as I simply seek you in this moment.
Let me delight in the way you have called your people to live—
according to your law of love, and with all attention to the now. Amen.

His invisible attributes, namely, his eternal power and divine nature,
have been clearly perceived, ever since the creation of the world,
in the things that have been made.
Romans 1:20 (ESV)

THE LOVELY HIDDEN ONE

Worthy are you, our Lord and God, to receive glory and honor and power,
for you created all things, and by your will they existed and were created.
Revelation 4:11 (ESV)

Close your eyes, and remember your first pangs of love. Remember your awe at the beauty of my world.

Remember when you stood as a child by the morning banks of the river and saw the mists dance, when you leaned over the tenement balcony and heard sweet laughter from your neighbor. Remember when you watched stars rise over the desert, so bright you thought each must be the sun of another world. Remember when a song first made you weep. Remember when you realized how truly you loved someone because you had lost them. Remember when you saw the face of your friend and knew you would die for them, when the garden your mother planted flourished with poppies, and when your grandfather put you on his knee and told you the story of your brave pilgrim family.

Remember when you saw Jesus clearly and knew that a single day with him was worth your very life.

I remember, Lord. It nearly makes me weep.

As all true beauty should. I showed myself to you in all of this. What you loved most deeply loved you back, perfect and whole and calling you to come and live as part of my own hidden beauty.

So when the wild-haired storm shakes itself above you, listen for my love in the rushing rain. I show myself to you in all the holy riot of the world.

Lord, you are the source and creator of all goodness and beauty.
Teach me to see you in the things you have made, and teach me
to know and love you by living vibrantly in your creation. Amen.

The seed on good soil stands for those with a noble and good heart,
who hear the word, retain it, and by persevering produce a crop.
Luke 8:15 (NIV)

THE NEEDED THING

"Martha, Martha," the Lord answered, "you are worried and upset
about many things, but few things are needed—or indeed only one.
Mary has chosen what is better, and it will not be taken away from her."
Luke 10:41–42 (NIV)

The life of God, of truth and understanding, lands in your heart with the fragility of a seed. It is possible it will wither, be crushed, be pecked and torn, be strangled by lies.

The same word is sowed to all. Christ the Sower shows no favoritism, respects no person above another. The truth is the truth, as a kernel of wheat is wheat indeed, and an acorn is only and always the seed of the ancient oak.

The human heart is a fickle field, rocky and weed-laden. Your own heart makes it hard for truth to take root. Too often you work when you ought to surrender, then give up when you ought to be working.

Your way is not easy, Lord.

It is better than easy. It is life.

What do I need to do?

Today, quiet your heart. Look inside. Consider the growth of the word in you. Where is your soil stony? Where do the birds ravage my tender promises to you? Where do the thorns and poisonous vines sprout?

Listening is the needed thing. Sit still at the feet of Christ. Silence fears. Cease frenzied activity. Stop your mouth. Breathe in the presence of the Quiet Planter. Listen to the voice of the one in whom is all truth and every understanding. You may keep whatever treasures you gather at the feet of your simple King.

Lord, you know that many things trouble me, from outside my heart and from
within it. Help me quiet myself today, to truly listen and receive your word,
allowing your truth to bear fruit in my life. Amen.

Do not put your trust in princes, in human beings, who cannot save.
Psalm 146:3 (NIV)

WHO?

It is better to take refuge in the LORD than to trust in humans.
Psalm 118:8 (NIV)

ـؤ

Who protects you?
Who provides for you?
Who hears your appeal?
Who works for your requests?
Who brings you justice?
Who fights for you?
Who is worthy of your faith?

You, Lord. I know it.

Then why do you not live like you believe it? Why do you live for so many others, who are only your sisters and brothers, instead of seeking your Father? You show your trust with your time, your money, and your belief.

How do I change?

Close your eyes and see the truth.
Repeat this in your heart:
There is no army strong enough to protect you,
no employer rich enough to provide for you,
no leader kind enough to hear you,
no servant sufficient to work for you,
no judge fair enough to be just for you,
no advocate willing to fight for you.
No one—no one, no one—worthy of your faith
can be found upon the earth or beneath it,
in this or any other nation,
in this or any other age.
Only me.
Trust me.

ـؤ

Lord, this world tempts me to place my faith in many other people. Help me see them only as the humans they are, and reserve my deepest trust for you alone. Amen.

He woke up and rebuked the wind, and said to the sea,
"Peace! Be still!" Then the wind ceased, and there was a dead calm.
Mark 4:39 (NRSV)

THE PEACEMAKER

Blessed are the peacemakers, for they will be called children of God.
Matthew 5:9 (NRSV)

I watch the masses rage in a vain boiling, like a storm that seeks to sink its master. They spit and curse. They would scald the whole world if they could.

All wounded things are angry and afraid. If you corner them, even if to draw the poison or pull the thorn, they will bite you.

Give us peace, Lord.

I have already given you peace, but not the world's kind. My peace holds paradoxes. Mine is the gentle embrace and the holy scourge. Mine is the breaking of the evil bow and the drawing of my own, bent wide as the sky, with an arrow like the sun.

The world is a field that must be plowed before it may be planted. Take pity on the stones that refuse to move for my blade, for they will be tossed aside. It may seem harsh, but that too is my peace. That too is my love.

At my word, you will not only lay down your weapons, you will melt them to make tools of plenty. You will not only cease to rage, you will begin to praise. I will turn the field of blood into a harvest of life, and you will be to me the thresher, the harvest, and the heir of the land. You shall be a child of peace.

Lord, your peace opposes the broken and violent systems of this world.
Help my heart love what you love and refuse the temptation
to cling to lies or conflict. Amen.

Know that the LORD is God.
It is he that made us, and we are his;
we are his people, and the sheep of his pasture.
Psalm 100:3 (NRSV)

H I S

Whether we live or whether we die, we are the Lord's.
Romans 14:8 (NRSV)

ـﯨﮉ

You belong to me, the work of my hands, the image of my living Son, the heir of creation, beloved.

You belong to me, the work of my hands, the image of my living Son, the heir of creation.

You belong to me, the work of my hands, the image of my living Son.

You belong to me, the work of my hands.

You belong to me.

You belong.

You.

ـﯨﮉ

Holy Father, you made me as part of your creation,
and you have remade me in Jesus Christ.
Help me believe I belong. Let me live as fully yours. Amen.

Sow for yourselves righteousness;
reap steadfast love;
break up your fallow ground;
for it is time to seek the LORD,
that he may come and rain righteousness upon you.

Hosea 10:12 (NRSV)

SEEK

Seek the LORD and his strength,
seek his presence continually.

1 Chronicles 16:11 (NRSV)

All your life, you have never truly known what you were looking for. As a child you thought it was love and acceptance. When that failed, you thought it was success or power. Then, when you still came up empty, it was beauty, a home, a different story. You tried pleasure and even truth. But none of those were right.

Then what am I looking for?

Listen to me. Plow the ground where you thought nothing could grow, and plant the seed I gave you. Give me your heart today, and again tomorrow—your whole heart, beating and full. I will come to stay with you and work the soil, and when you see me from afar, striding across the field, you'll know that you have found the only thing worth seeking.

Lord, you promise that your children will find every good thing
when they find you. Help me seek you and your kingdom,
trusting your promise that you will give your presence to me. Amen.

Ho, everyone who thirsts, come to the waters;
and you that have no money,
come, buy and eat!
Come, buy wine and milk
without money and without price.
Isaiah 55:1 (NRSV)

WITHOUT PRICE

Blessed are those who hunger and thirst for righteousness, for they will be filled.
Matthew 5:6 (NRSV)

If every store stood empty and the markets were dead, if the threshers went silent, the silos held only echoes, and if your neighbor's pantry was as bare as yours, where would you go for food?

Famine is a slow hunter. It gives you time to think. Time to keep looking, to keep hoping, to keep hungering. "Food for the belly, and the belly for food," they say, but what does that phrase mean on the day of starvation?

Lord, feed me.

The ravens by Elijah's creek flew where no one walked to bring bounty to the famished prophet. My messenger delivered bread to him as he slept beneath the juniper tree. The widow and her starving son laid their last loaf before him, in the most trusting kind of despair.

Every mother bird feeds her young, so why do you still think you have to buy my gifts with your righteousness? There is not money enough in all the world to buy a crumb of life from me. I do not sell. I only give.

Lord, feed me.

There are waters you cannot see and bread you cannot taste until you believe. Abundance is here, but it will not look like you think. My righteousness shall satisfy you. My holiness will be your nourishment.

I will sell you nothing, little bird. But I will give you everything.

Lord, you have provided for all who are willing to come to you. Please help me
trust you not only for my salvation, but for my daily righteousness,
looking to you to satisfy all my needs. Amen.

11

In every situation, by prayer and petition,
with thanksgiving, present your requests to God.
Philippians 4:6 (NIV)

JUST ASK

You may ask me for anything in my name, and I will do it.
John 14:14 (NIV)

⟡

The hesitation you feel in prayer is not faith.
What you feel
    keeps in place mountains
    that ought to be moved.
You do not have because you do not ask.
You do not know because you do not ask.
You do not stay faithful to my word because you do not ask.
You do not see my kingdom come or my will done because you
    do not ask.

    Lord, is that really true?

Must I say more?
Come to me in faith.
Demand nothing, but ask all,
    never doubting that I give good gifts—
    the best of all simply my eternal promise
    to always, always hear you.

⟡

Lord, I believe that you hear me and that you are good.
Please give me faith to approach you humbly with all my requests
in thanksgiving and graciousness, allowing you to provide for me
and the world I am called to intercede for. Amen.

There is no fear in love. But perfect love drives out fear,
because fear has to do with punishment. The one who fears
is not made perfect in love.

1 John 4:18 (NIV)

FEARLESS

So do not fear, for I am with you; do not be dismayed,
for I am your God. I will strengthen you and help you;
I will uphold you with my righteous right hand.

Isaiah 41:10 (NIV)

Fear is doubt.

Love kills doubt.

I am love.

Father, you are perfect love, the enemy of all my fears.
Help me cling to you in trust and faith,
believing in your goodness and mercy. Amen.

I sought the LORD, and he answered me,
and delivered me from all my fears.
Look to him, and be radiant;
so your faces shall never be ashamed.
Psalm 34:4–5 (NRSV)

A RADIANT HOPE

Hope does not put us to shame,
because God's love has been poured out into our hearts.
Romans 5:5 (NIV)

The whole world seeks to make you ashamed—of who you are, of what you have done, of all you have not done.

Shame is the leverage of hell. It is the cruelest kind of condemnation because it begins inside your own heart. All your life, shame has stalked you.

Shame is fear wearing a righteous mask. It would have no power over you if you were not afraid. You are afraid to be seen as naked, so you cover yourself. You are afraid to be seen as weak, so you work till you bleed to show how strong you are. You are afraid—not to be poor, but to be seen as poor; not to be alone, but to be seen as lonely; not to die, but for others to see you dying.

You know me so well.

Hope crushes shame, for hope crushes fear. Love is a radiant hope for those who seek me. All along the way that leads east from Eden, there are stories of the One who chose weakness, who embraced poverty, who walked through the streets stripped naked by the cruelty of the world, all uncovered, all laid bare, and yet all radiant.

And all hopeful.
And all unashamed.

You can join him. You can know what it is for shame to be crushed by radiance.

Lord, shame does not come from you. Let your perfect love in Jesus
cast out all my fear. Help me reject shame to see myself as you see me. Amen.

And when you turn to the right or when you turn to the left,
your ears shall hear a word behind you, saying,
"This is the way; walk in it."
Isaiah 30:21 (NRSV)

STRANGE WAY

Jesus said to him, "I am the way, and the truth, and the life.
No one comes to the Father except through me."
John 14:6 (NRSV)

Beloved wanderer, walk this way.
Follow Christ, your Prophet, Priest, and King,
    your Way, Truth, and Life.
Walk until the silence of this road becomes true listening.

> *How do I walk well?*

Pay attention to all you see, and fall in love with none of it,
    except for what you see me in.
Then, ponder this riddle for a mile or two:
"Who leads the one who refuses to be led?"

> *Oh, guide me.*

Look ahead of you, where the narrow trail lifts to the horizon—
    see that man who carries nothing a traveler should carry?

> *I think I see him.*

His is the strange and eternal Way.
He is made of Earth and Air, dust of Humanity and Spirit of God.
He is the Road and the First Walker,
    both the Pilgrim and the Lord of the Kingdom Sought.

Follow him.
Come home.

Lord, you guide all souls that seek you, rewarding the diligence
of those hungry for life. Please help me know and follow Jesus,
and so find guidance for all my life in him. Amen.

15

The light has come into the world, and people loved the darkness
rather than the light because their deeds were evil.
John 3:19 (ESV)

FROM THE DARKNESS

For you were once darkness, but now you are light in the Lord.
Live as children of light.
Ephesians 5:8 (NIV)

～ᴡ

Everything you see in this world is a sign of something beyond it. Yes, darkness too. Today, the morning crept with the rising sun. The light found you, and shadows fled—for where light is, darkness cannot stay.

Is your heart prepared for my perfect light? Is your life ready for full exposure?

Or would you prefer a few shadows?

I'd rather not say.

Ah! Darkness, there. It cannot last, you know. It is not good to cling to shadows, for you may find that shadows cling to you. You flee from my full light. You cannot bear it. What are you afraid I will see?

Must I say?

Yes, or I will say it. And trust me—it will be better to leave the darkness of your own choice than to make me pull you from the shadows. Do not doubt that I will. I love you too much to leave you in any darkness. Leave the dark behind. Become who you are: a child of the Father of Lights.

～ᴡ

Lord, you are the light of the world. In you is no darkness at all.
Grant in your mercy that I may be brought fully into your light,
living in the perfect love that casts out all fear. Amen.

But whoever does what is true comes to the light,
so that it may be clearly seen that his works have been carried out in God.
John 3:21 (ESV)

INTO THE LIGHT

You are all children of the light and children of the day.
We do not belong to the night or to the darkness.
1 Thessalonians 5:5 (NIV)

In the beginning, I called light into existence, and it was very good. Nothing has changed. To this day, rays shine forth from me, the very light of very light, and are echoed in all creation—from the farthest star to the lamp on your table.

How beautiful the light is.

Yes, how beautiful. How life-giving, and how dangerous. A laser can slice diamond, and the soft flame of a candle, with its perfect warmth, is the fire of suns. All this I call very good. And you I call good, too—with all my children of light.

Those who walk in my light shine.

I want to walk in your light.

Then today you face a choice. To be is wonderful, to be faithful more wonderful still. Act in accordance with your nature in Jesus, the light of the world. His love is light, for my love is light. Walk in your belonging, clearly seen, so that what you do, like the lamp set high in a dark room, may be visible to all with eyes to see.

I praise you, Father—creator of all good things, giver of all good gifts.
Grant that the strength and brightness of Jesus be my light,
and that I may shine with him, as a reflection of your glory. Amen.

Without faith it is impossible to please Him, for he who comes to God must believe that He is, and that He is a rewarder of those who diligently seek Him.
Hebrews 11:6 (NRSV)

WITH ALL DILIGENCE

Seek and you will find.
Matthew 7:7 (NIV)

‿ﹶﻭ

Where are you, Lord?

[silence]

Why do you make this so hard?

[silence]

Look, I'm trying. I want to know you, to love Christ with all I have and am, to live in the light.

[silence]

I have knocked! I have looked!
For years, with tears,
and barely glimpsed you at the best of times.
I have asked many questions that have never been answered, like why this? Where are you?

[silence]

I barely remember why, but I believe, Lord.
Still, help my unbelief.

I am.
Beloved, what is easily gained is little loved.
My promise stands.
You have always been held by the one you searched for.
My gift is the diligent seeking, and your eternal reward will be me.

‿ﹶﻭ

Father, you have promised that you will be found by all who look for you.
Please grant me diligence—no matter whether finding you is quick
and easy or long and difficult. Help me trust, and grow my faith
in your presence and goodness. Amen.

Has the Lᴏʀᴅ as great delight in burnt offerings and sacrifices, as in
obedience to the voice of the Lᴏʀᴅ? Surely, to obey is better than sacrifice.
1 Samuel 15:22 (Nʀsv)

AT THE ALTAR OF LIFE

From him and through him and to him are all things.
To him be the glory forever. . . . I appeal to you therefore, brothers and sisters,
by the mercies of God, to present your bodies as a living sacrifice,
holy and acceptable to God, which is your spiritual worship.
Romans 11:36–12:1 (Nʀsv)

ﮞ

Quiet your heart; slow your breathing.
Place two fingers on your wrist or the vein that throbs below your jaw.
Feel the beating blood, pumped under your skin like the rivers of life
that once flowed from my own emerald Eden.

I feel my heart beat.

For your beating life, the Carpenter of Israel gave his own.
The world stretched him across two rough boards
and fixed him there with nails that did not spare his flesh
any more than they spared the wood on the other side.
Those two boards became an eternal door for those who knock.

Blood was given for blood. Skin for skin.
Not because I was evil in my justice or a God hungry for pain,
but because for your kind to listen to the point of life
Jesus had to listen to the point of death.

Now, sacrifice for sacrifice!
You who were bought with innocent blood, stand before me.
Sacrifice yourself—not until you die,
but until you come to life,
and breathe and feel your heart beat
and live and obey,
and, in this place of holy blood, find love.

ﮞ

Lord, in Jesus you sacrificed all precious things to gain a kingdom of sons and
daughters. Help me fully obey you, as a living sacrifice to your goodness. Amen.

Indeed, the whole earth is mine,
but you shall be for me a priestly kingdom and a holy nation.
Exodus 19:5–6 (NRSV)

BEFORE THE MOUNTAIN

But you are a chosen race, a royal priesthood, a holy nation,
God's own people, in order that you may proclaim the mighty acts of him
who called you out of darkness into his marvelous light.
1 Peter 2:9 (NRSV)

Prepare yourself, for you are called to serve me today, to carry the prayers of your people before me and worship in my presence.

> *Me? I am no priest. I can barely get my own life together.*
> *I'd probably drop the candle and burn the place down.*

Have you forgotten what consecrates my servants? Blood, oil, and the clean garment—all things that came from beyond you, given to you by Father, Son, and Spirit.

Do not stay where you are when you hear the call to come. Draw near to me. Come before me like a child and say only, "Here I am." That is how you rise to the occasion—how the impossible mountain humbles itself to welcome you.

> *Here I am.*

Here you may be with me.

Lord, you have given all your people access to your presence and authority
in worship and prayer so that we might experience you fully and bring others
before you in love. Help me understand and embrace my own life as
a priest before you, living holy and focused on your presence. Amen.

OF CLAY

We have this treasure in clay jars, so that it may be made clear that this
extraordinary power belongs to God and does not come from us.
2 Corinthians 4:7 (NRSV)

Though you are only a piece of earth
a few years shy of crumbling,
you are beloved.

You, who I cast upon the wheel,
shaping you as the disc beneath you spun,
my fingers stained by your ruddy hue,
my prints left upon the vessel which takes more shape every day.

It is my will to fill the imperfect with perfection,
to put my Spirit within your spirit,
to bring you to life with my own life,
to glaze rough clay with infinity,
to heat you until you gleam like opal in the heart of the kiln,
dancing in heat and laughing with the kind and leaping flames.

You, beloved piece of earth, are far from done,
but already you are treasured.

> *All of this care, this love, this strong kindness—*
> *what do you see in me?*

Myself.

Father, you are the one who has fashioned my life, and placed your
Spirit within me. Let me surrender to your process of shaping me and live
in awe and wonder of what you are doing in my life. Amen.

But as he who called you is holy, you also be holy in all
your conduct, since it is written, "You shall be holy, for I am holy."
1 Peter 1:15–16 (ESV)

HOLY, HOLY, HOLY

In the center, around the throne . . . the four living creatures had six wings
and were covered with eyes all around, even under [their] wings. Day and night
they never stop saying: "Holy, holy, holy is the Lord God Almighty,
who was, and is, and is to come."
Revelation 4:6–8 (NIV)

Heaven is not far away. Its mystery burns behind everything, like a lamp behind a curtained window. My presence is here, and you may enter it at any time. How I long to be close to you! My child, be in awe today. Be reverent, for this earth is holy. I am holy. Do not take your access to my presence for granted, nor despise your welcome as my perfect child in the place of utter Light.

I long to see you.

I am here. This is my eternal promise for you to hold anew today: soon you will know as you are known. Not merely a knowing of the mind, but a knowing of your deepest being, where to simply be is to be set apart and mere existence becomes worship.

What does this mean?

That in Jesus my holiness is yours. That today can become heaven.

How, Father?

Kiss the Son, then follow him.
Know holy. Be holy. Do holy.

Let living be your act of worship. In this you join the hosts in endless praise and will hear, in their rhythmic song, my everlasting name, rising in the voice of the holy ones. Rising in your voice.

Lord of Heaven, you are all holiness, all perfection. In you is no darkness. You
are all goodness. Complete light. Today, help me to be set apart for your worship
in all that I do and say, to be truly holy as you, my God, are holy. Amen.

To what will I compare this generation?
It is like children sitting in the marketplaces and calling to one another,
"We played the flute for you, and you did not dance;
we wailed, and you did not mourn."
Matthew 11:16–17 (NRSV)

CHILDREN OF HARMONY

Rejoice with those who rejoice; mourn with those who mourn.
Live in harmony with one another.
Romans 12:15–16 (NIV)

꙼

When the Son of Man walked among the villages, the self-righteous believed he couldn't do a single thing right.

He worked on the Sabbath. "How dare he," they said. He raised the dead, which so-called "civilized" people preferred be tidily buried according to proper etiquette. He ate when he should have fasted, and then, when he went without a meal or two, the "respectable" folk spat, and gossiped, and called him possessed. Those "good" people wiped their mouths, then stalked home to gaze into their mirrors and whisper to their image, "How responsible you are! How righteous! How good it is that you are in the world to keep such fools as he from trashing the place!"

Lord, help me not be like that.

Then dance when Christ sings, and grieve when you see him weeping. Jesus is rejected ten thousand times a day, even by those who call themselves his disciples. Is there a place in your life you'd rather he did not go? Repent, before he demands it of you. Is there a place in the world you think unworthy of the feet of Jesus? Walk there first, and upend whatever brokenness you find with the truth and with my kindness and with a love that spares no one—least of all the "good."

Least of all, yourself.

꙼

Lord, in Jesus you have changed the world, putting to shame all hypocrites.
Help me live in the power and discernment of Jesus, not in appearances,
but in reality, all for your glory. Amen.

No good tree bears bad fruit, nor again does a bad tree bear good fruit,
for each tree is known by its own fruit.
Luke 6:43–44 (ESV)

THE FRUITBEARERS

But the fruit of the Spirit is love, joy, peace, patience, kindness, goodness,
faithfulness, gentleness, self-control; against such things there is no law.
Galatians 5:22–23 (ESV)

ے

The branches are laden, bowing with fruit. The harvest is near.
Today, I will walk the orchard, inspecting every branch, to see what
    I may expect of them.
Good fruit or bad? A rich crop or sparse? Blight? Worms? Mildew?
Perhaps, if it is good, a fivefold bounty—
    or twentyfold, or one hundredfold!

Father, what will you find on me?

What do you think I will find on you?
Everything bears according to its nature, reproducing fruit after its kind.
You know the fruit I desire: the kind I myself bear.
For I am the Great Tree, you a branch.

I want to be fruitful.

Then feel the strength flowing from my roots.
Be upright, a true child of mine.
Today, be fully grafted into me—bark of my bark, sap of my sap.
Let me purify your heart. Let me prune you, cutting away all that weakens,
    all that causes rot.

Do it, Father—even if it hurts.

I have already begun. You will be abundant. A good branch.
The hungry will thrive on our fruit:
Love. Joy. Peace. Patience. Kindness. Goodness. Faithfulness. Gentleness.
    Self-control.

ے

Dear Father, you have made me in your image and remade me
through the blood of Jesus and the sanctification of the Holy Spirit.
Help me live in fruitfulness, showing the world your abundance. Amen.

Like a lion—so He breaks all my bones,
from day until night You make an end of me.
Isaiah 38:13 (NASB)

THE BONESETTER

Make me to hear joy and gladness,
Let the bones which You have broken rejoice.
Psalm 51:8 (NASB)

◞

My poor, beloved child. You are sliced and bruised. Bleeding. Cracked.
Where did this harm come from? Who made these wounds? That scar—
how long has it darkened your face? It must have hurt to drag that leg
behind you, exhausting to hide it from those you feared. It pains me to
see you like this today. I know how gashes hurt.

You do?

Yes.
The road behind you is dark with blood. It is not good for you to go on yet.

What, then?

Much good, in the end. But a little more pain before the good.

Why?

You think yourself healed. That's the problem. Doesn't it trouble you that
you cannot run? You hid when you were hurt. You should have called for
me. Now your bones are crooked. They healed wrong.

Oh, help me!

I will.
Look here. See me. Healing begins today. Feel my hands upon the limb. You
must let me break you afresh before true healing comes. It will hurt, but I
will hold you. I will set the bones straight, and soon we will run together.

◞

Lord, all your works toward us are good—even the ones that are painful.
Let me trust your goodness today, offering you the parts of my life
I have not yet allowed you to touch. Be gentle as you restore me.
Help my belief in your goodness stand firm. Amen.

Praise be to the God and Father of our Lord Jesus Christ, the Father of compassion and the God of all comfort, who comforts us in all our troubles, so that we can comfort those in any trouble with the comfort we ourselves receive from God.
2 Corinthians 1:3–4 (NIV)

OF ALL COMFORT

Blessed are those who mourn, for they will be comforted.
Matthew 5:4 (NRSV)

مـرو

I too have wept.
I too have lost.
I too have heard the sentence of injustice
    pronounced over my head.
I too have known hunger,
    and lack,
    and prison.
I too have fled the cruel,
    have seen friends flee,
    have heard the rumors,
    have been mocked.
I too have been handed over to torturers,
    have seen my own
    martyred like sheep,
have felt the ship sinking under my feet.
I too have been kept from my beloved,
    have seen my lover in the arms of my enemy–and enjoying it.

I too have seen the grave.
I too have lost
    everything.
All this is true. I swear it by my own name.
And I am here to say two things:
It will all be made right,
    and you were never alone.

مـرو

Lord, you have known, through the sufferings of Christ and your people, every kind of mourning. Please grant comfort to all those who need it, for you are the God of all consolation. Thank you–thank you, thank you. Amen.

See, I am doing a new thing! Now it springs up; do you not perceive it?
I am making a way in the wilderness and streams in the wasteland.
Isaiah 43:19 (NIV)

DEEPER WELLS

Jesus answered, " . . . Whoever drinks the water I give them
will never thirst. Indeed, the water I give them
will become in them a spring of water welling up to eternal life."
John 4:13–14 (NIV)

The desert is a skeleton. Bone dry. Thirsty. Look at it. Can you dream such a wilderness could one day look like Eden?

Can this place live?

Of course. So it was with your soul. But I merely spoke, and life began to flow. A trickle at first, for such is my way, but the flood is coming.

I still thirst, Lord.

Today, drink deeply of the water, filling the barren cracks of your life, no matter how hopeless things look. Carry this truth in the secret place of your soul: in my provision you can be fully satisfied and yet always thirsty for more of me, always longing for the deeper streams.

You can live in an oasis ringed by thirst and famine. See these waters rush? Smell their freshness. Hear their bubbling cascade.

This place was once the floor of a great river, and it will be again. For I am carving a path for water. In you, through you. Streams in the wild emptiness, which will nourish a garden planted before the enemy.

My springs flow up to you from wells dug deeper than the world.

Father, you are the source of all life and goodness.
You provide perfectly for our needs. Please help me trust in your
abundance and wait patiently for the full expression of your love in my life,
trusting in Jesus Christ, the Water of Life. Amen.

The LORD is near to the brokenhearted,
and saves the crushed in spirit.
Psalm 34:18 (NRSV)

EMPTY-HANDED

Blessed are the poor in spirit, for theirs is the kingdom of heaven.
Matthew 5:3 (NRSV)

ـس

Not everyone who has nothing
   knows they have nothing.
There is no poverty so profound as
   thinking nothing is something.
The one who thinks their empty cup is full
   will drink air for a lifetime—
always thirsting,
   never asking me for water.

Did I see you down in the field
   counting pebbles as if they were coins?
Did I see you playing president
   over a congress of dust?

I see you take,
I see you give,
   and I long for you to know yourself as poor,
   for then you might know me as rich.
Only then will you come farther into the kingdom,
   where I am so close to the crushed and broken
   that I dare you to tell us apart.

     Lord, let me know myself,
     and let me humble myself,
     and let me draw near to you,
     that I, too, might be perfect in your poor richness.

ـس

Lord, you have called the poor in spirit your own and have humbled
those who think themselves rich. Let me see my empty cup
for what it is and love you for it. Amen.

A person may think their own ways are right,
but the LORD weighs the heart.

Proverbs 21:2 (NIV)

UNJUSTIFICATION

Wanting to justify himself, he asked Jesus,
"And who is my neighbor?"

Luke 10:29 (NRSV)

How many times have you walked past the wounded, the poor, the forgotten, the unclean? How many times have you moved to the other side of the road—the other side of the world—and felt nothing but righteous about ignoring the least and the lost?

> *I was—*
> *I thought—*
> *I mean—*

Be silent. Listen. There is no excuse. There is only your heart, weighed in my balances and found wanting in compassion, after receiving a love deeper than time.

Can you justify that?

Lord, you neglect no one, and your love is abundant for all who are suffering.
Forgive my own callous heart, and lead me to true compassion,
showing others the love I have myself been given. Amen.

God is my helper; the Lord is the upholder of my life.
Psalm 54:4 (NRSV)

THE HELP

We can say with confidence, "The Lord is my helper;
I will not be afraid. What can anyone do to me?"
Hebrews 13:6 (NRSV)

ﱞ

I want to see the world as you do, Father.

Then you must shun fear.

I am more constant than the land, older than the seas by infinite ages. I am the one without beginning, to whom Time tells every secret. Stay by my side, for I will stay by yours, perfect help for every weakness.

In your chest, a muscle the size of your fist sends blood rushing down the red roads of your flesh.

It was my finger that set it ticking, before you ever saw light outside your mother. During the days of its beating, not a thump goes unnoticed. It quickens in danger or in love. It slows in rest. It aches, burdened by ill news or hard work. It will be my finger that hushes it at last and lays it to sleep for a while. Even that will not mean I have left you.

Why do you care for us? We are so small.

When will you stop thinking that up is higher than down? I am the keeper of every soul, the Father of all. I am the spinner of stars, the painter of every planet, and the weaver of your own hair. Do not think me too great for anything.

There is a humility that is royal, a meekness that only I am permitted. Your race calls it "help."

If you must fear something, fear forgetting that.

ﱞ

Lord, you are the infinite Creator, yet you choose to help every one of your people,
caring for our lives and well-being according to your will and wisdom.
Help me see and know your work in my life. Amen.

Rejoice in the Lord always. I will say it again: Rejoice!
Philippians 4:4 (NIV)

INEXPRESSIBLE

*Even though you do not see him now, you believe in him
and are filled with an inexpressible and glorious joy.*
1 Peter 1:8 (NIV)

There is a love beyond words, and you can know it.

It is beyond rationality, beyond explanation, beyond capture by thought or by art. You feel it as joy. You remember when you felt it first—that quickening of your spirit, the rush of emotion you couldn't explain. The lightness of it! It could not be described, but you knew it nonetheless. You knew me through it.

I remember!

You have felt it since, at one moment or another, bursting into your life like fireworks. You know when and how. I know why.

Joy is light—a beam from a source you cannot see that warms and brightens and makes alive. Joy is the knowing that leaps between parent and child. It doesn't need words, for the baby has none. It is a love of being, of closeness, of provision. It is a love of comfort, and this-is-good, and being held, and a love of holding, too, and of soothing. It is my love for you.

Did you know joy can be chosen? The feeling is but the branches of a thing whose roots lie deep within your being.

Blessed are you who have not seen and yet believe, for in holy irrationality you chose a truth that, like joy, cannot be fully understood. So too can you choose to celebrate life itself, regardless of circumstances. You can know my joy beyond any need to talk about it.

I want to live this way!

Then choose. Rejoice! Rejoice! Again I say it to you, for today: Rejoice!

Lord, you are the source of all happiness and all contentment, all celebration and all joy. Please help me live into your joy, which is beyond words, choosing it again and again until it becomes my nature, as it has always been yours. Amen.

The LORD takes pleasure in his people.

Psalm 149:4 (ESV)

WELL PLEASED

And just as he was coming up out of the water, he saw the heavens torn apart and the Spirit descending like a dove on him. And a voice came from heaven, "You are my Son, the Beloved; with you I am well pleased."

Mark 1:10–11 (NRSV)

⁓

When you heard me call your name today, did you feel happy or afraid? Did you think I came to punish you or to play? Every father's voice can make a name mean many things. One tone accuses, another praises.

What did you hear?

I don't know.

I know.

You know my love, but you do not believe I like you. You do not believe I take pleasure in you. Do you know I see my Son in you? In him, you are my wonderful adopted, my beloved child.

Hear me say it again: you are my beloved child.

True of Jesus eternally, true of you today.

There is no fear in perfect love, so why do you look for me over your shoulder when all I wish is for you to see yourself as I see you?

I want to see myself your way!

Then I will help your unbelief. Beyond anything you could do, I love you. Because you merely are—my own beloved, washed in the great river, my Spirit sealing you, looking up, making the heart of your Father well, well pleased.

⁓

Father, you have drawn me and your whole Church to your son Jesus and named us as your beloved through him. Help me know your pleasure today, and may that happy love lead me to live in holiness and praise of you. Amen.

All my bones shall say, "O LORD, who is like you?
You deliver the weak from those too strong for them,
the weak and needy from those who despoil them."
Psalm 35:10 (NRSV)

DELIVERANCE

The kings of the Gentiles lord it over them; and those in authority over them
are called benefactors. But not so with you; rather the greatest among you
must become like the youngest, and the leader like one who serves.
Luke 22:25–26 (NRSV)

It is the way of the proud to think they have won
    when the truth is they did not recognize the moment of their defeat.
The rich gloat. The strong boast.
They hurt the defenseless and think they get away with it.
But all that is done to the weak is done to my Son.
Their beatings, his bruises.
Their wounds, his bleeding.
Their robbery, his loss.
The wicked are cruel, but the watching Father is just.
I am waiting for the right moment.

    I am waiting too, Lord. Help me be like Jesus.

If that is your wish, then think of this:
    to deliver the world, it only took one man,
    clothed like a homeless servant,
    who listened to his Father and said,
    "Your way, not mine."
Do you dare join him down in the dust of power?

    Help me, Lord.

It is the way of the meek to think they have lost
    when the truth is they did not recognize the moment of their victory.

Lord, in Jesus you have turned the way of the world upside down.
Let me walk in his way, close to the poor and helpless, waiting eagerly for
your kingdom to set our many wrongs right. Defend all the weak. Amen.

Give careful thought to the paths for your feet and be steadfast in all your ways.
Do not turn to the right or the left; keep your foot from evil.
Proverbs 4:26–27 (NIV)

THE GOOD PATH

Wide is the gate and broad is the road that leads to destruction,
and many enter through it. But small is the gate and narrow
the road that leads to life, and only a few find it.
Matthew 7:13–14 (NIV)

Walking a long road is like this: you cannot see where you are going until you are nearly there. Life is like that, too. You will live much more than you'd like before you can see who you are becoming.

Child, did you lay the foundation of this road of life? Did you blaze the trail of salvation? Is your wisdom so great that you know where to place your feet? Your kind gets lost so easily.

Then how do I walk, Father?

Trust me.

Do not trust the way things appear. Do not trust the voices off the path, for they will try to sell you lies. Do not trust that good will always seem good, or that evil will always seem evil. Do not trust your own feet.

Today, surrender your false sense of direction. I will give you a map and compass, which are my Word and wisdom. My Spirit will guide you, and my light will lead you home. Narrow, the good path seems, until you see it as I do—widening just beyond your sight, until life is as broad as heaven.

Lord, you have not asked me to do anything that Jesus has not done first.
Let me follow him in holiness, dedicated to the path you have shown us through him.
Help me hear and heed your guidance, allowing your Word,
your Church, and your Spirit to lead me in the way of Christ. Amen.

Then His disciples remembered that it was written,
"Zeal for Your house has eaten Me up."
John 2:17 (NKJV)

THE ZEALOT

Like living stones, let yourselves be built into a spiritual house,
to be a holy priesthood, to offer spiritual sacrifices
acceptable to God through Jesus Christ.
1 Peter 2:5 (NRSV)

Let it burn,
the flame in the bone
that is the seed of a word from
    me.
Let it eat you
from the heart to the tongue to
    the hands
in a holy consuming
single purpose,
like the clarity of new wine
that moves across the lips
of those who have been asleep.
Let it burn,
your love for my house,
the stones set on Christ which
    frame a temple
large enough for every nation.
This is home!
This is the city on the hill of God!

This is the lampstand in a dark
    room,
upon which are seven flames.
This is my anointed Church.
The maw of hell shall fall silent
    before her,
the teeth of evil loose in their
    sockets.

Lord, I yearn for your glory.

Let it burn,
the Spirit in your flesh,
rustling like the leaves of the tree
    of life,
which are for healing.
This place is the perfect future.
This place is the dwelling of the
    redeemed.
This place is home.
Come, and be ever my own.

Lord, you have founded your Church on Jesus Christ and called to its
people from every nation of earth. Awaken my love for your body, and help me
humbly serve my brothers and sisters in faith with gladness and a pure heart,
through the power of your Spirit. Amen.

He has shown you, O mortal, what is good.
And what does the LORD require of you? To act justly and
to love mercy and to walk humbly with your God.
Micah 6:8 (NIV)

HE HAS SHOWN US

You shall love the Lord your God with all your heart and with all your
soul and with all your mind. This is the great and first commandment.
And a second is like it: You shall love your neighbor as yourself.
On these two commandments depend all the Law and the Prophets.
Matthew 22:37–40 (ESV)

Today, this is what I want from you: I want you to be like me.

Such an easy thing to hear, yet the hardest in the world to do.

All your life you've been told you must live for pleasure, for production, for prestige. Lies. You must live for love. To love and be loved by your God and your neighbor.

Father, help me.

I have already done better. I have shown you. If you have seen Jesus, you have seen me. Learn through him that I require everything—everything you have, everything you know, everything you do, everything you are.

It feels like so much.

It is. I know, because I have given it, too. Today, turn your being toward Jesus: seek justice, choosing right, no matter the cost. Grant mercy, loving freely, no matter why you shouldn't. Be humble, knowing the greatest in my kingdom is the servant of all.

I am the greatest because I am the First Servant. I have given everything. And today, that is what I want from you.

Lord, all good gifts come from you. Show me the parts of my life
I am holding back. Help me desire to be like you—
one who loves with everything. Let me live this day as an offering,
a gift of love to you through Jesus. Amen.

*"Behold, the days are coming," declares the Lord G*OD,
"when I will send a famine on the land—not a famine of bread,
*nor a thirst for water, but of hearing the words of the L*ORD*."*
Amos 8:11 (ESV)

FEAST AND FAMINE

But Jesus answered, "It is written, 'Man shall not live by bread alone,
but by every word that comes from the mouth of God.'"
Matthew 4:4 (ESV)

Come and eat! Feast with me today, out here in the desert—days from
water, weeks from shelter. There is bread and wine and meat. Good
meat. I am throwing a party, and everyone is invited. Right now there is
laughter at the table, rising from a host of happy misfits who revel in the
meal, for they know what starving tastes like. You do not know the value
of my words until you have known true hunger for them.

I must pay you for this.

I have nothing for sale.

Nothing is free.

It is costly for me, but I am rich. My abundance is enough for the whole
world, for all who will have me feed them. Sit, while I break bread, and
know me better. I want to be with you, to feast with you, to provide for
you and love you today, as your true Father.

But do not be surprised if my bread changes in your mouth to pure love,
and my wine to the water of life, and the laughter of this table to the
voice of the Spirit. Do not be surprised to find this feast, in the midst of
the world's famine, turn to the high and holy wedding table of my Son.

Father, all abundance is yours. You love fellowship, knowing and celebrating
with others, sharing freely and joyfully. Today, may I fully enjoy
your provision—whether it appears to be little or much.
Let me know the joy of living life as a feast with you. Amen.

There was Dagon, fallen on his face on the ground before the ark of the LORD!
His head and hands had been broken off and were lying on the threshold.
1 Samuel 5:4 (NIV)

WHOSE IS THIS TEMPLE?

We are in him who is true, in his Son Jesus Christ. He is the true God
and eternal life. Little children, keep yourselves from idols.
1 John 5:20–21 (ESV)

⁓

Come in, my child! The scent of prayer rises with sweet smoke in the temple today, and lamplight flickers among the curtains. What is holy here is yours, for you belong to the Holy One. Behind that veil, Christ the Priest walked, the Son of God, the Son of Man, the Eternal Life. You can walk there, too, for his sacrifice is yours. He makes you holy.

Wait. What is this? What are you carrying?

I don't want to say.

Whose is this stone face? These wooden hands? An idol? What is in your heart that you would make this and love it and give your life to it?

I don't want to say.

Look at me. Whose is this temple? To whom do you belong, body and mind?

Yours, Father. To you.

Must I share you with another? Must you live your life serving something else?

Deliver me.

Leave your idols in my presence. All of them. Stack them over there, as kindling before the fiery altar. Forsake them.

I will give where they have only taken. I will love where they have only hated. I will make you whole, and I will leave the gods you have served facedown and broken on my threshold before the perfect dawn.

⁓

Lord, you hate all false gods who lead your people astray.
Help me destroy whatever in my life that competes for your place. Amen.

38

It is the LORD your God who goes with you;
he will not fail you or forsake you.

Deuteronomy 31:6 (NRSV)

UNFORSAKEN

He has said, "I will never leave you or forsake you."
Hebrews 13:5 (NRSV)

~ـﻭ

Love is the enemy of fear.
I know you are afraid today, but do not seek courage.
Instead, hold to love, which is to say, hold on to me.

When you walk forward, you will find me already around the bend.
If you turn, you will find me behind you on the path.
In the dark I keep every watch beside the fire.
In the day I am the unblinking, the kind watchman.

Love is the enemy of fear.

Whose is the wide world?
Whose is the field? The desert?
Whose is the forest?
And the spirits of the forest?
And the beasts of the forest?
Whose is the sea?

All yours, Father.

I am the Un-leaver, you the Unforsaken.
Our journey is long, but it will prove my love, lest you ever be tempted
to deny it.
Say the truth, and be at peace.

Love is the enemy of fear.

~ـﻭ

Lord, you have promised to never leave or forsake your people.
Let me know your promise and learn faithfulness by watching you.
Rather than muster courage, help me hold to love. Amen.

They who wait for the LORD shall renew their strength; they shall mount up with wings like eagles; they shall run and not be weary; they shall walk and not faint.
Isaiah 40:31 (ESV)

WAIT

We do not lose heart. Though our outer self is wasting away, yet our inner self is being renewed day by day.
2 Corinthians 4:16 (NIV)

Wait.

Wait?

Wait.

But I—

Wait.

This is my promise for you today: you were chosen by me, from all the things you might have been, to be what you are becoming. You were known to me before the world was made, and you were loved. Before your earliest ancestor, I set a place for you at my table. Before your first weakness, I gave you all my strength.

So wait.

Taste the bread of renewal.

You belong to the sky, with the fiercest birds, your wings a testament to my power. You belong to the ground, with miles behind you, as you sprint without weariness. You belong to the fields and hills and cities, the paths no match for your endurance.

But I am weak.

I did not say you were not weak. I see you waste away as years march on. But with the wasting comes the waiting, and today, if you wait, you will feel flow from me the rush of heaven's life.

Lord, you are the source of all true strength. You are the one with the power to renew me—body, spirit, and mind. I pray that you will help my heart remember the truth of your might and your promise to show your strength in my weakness. Amen.

Do not let your hands hang limp.
The LORD your God is with you,
the Mighty Warrior who saves.
He will take great delight in you;
in his love he will no longer rebuke you,
but will rejoice over you with singing.
Zephaniah 3:16–17 (NIV)

TO LIFT THE HANDS

I will bless you as long as I live;
I will lift up my hands and call on your name.
Psalm 63:4 (NRSV)

Holy Father, eternal God,
I bring my praise to you today, my hands held out.
You know me and all that is in me—
both what reflects you and what desperately needs refining.
With all you have given me,
though it may be only a little,
I bless you.

Welcome to my presence.
I sing over you the songs of holy war,
words of salvation that heal the brokenhearted.

These hands you have given me, I lift before you.
They were withered once, useless.
But you healed them with a word
when you asked me to stretch them before you in faith.
What once was sadness you have made into strength.
What once was weakness you have made into joy.
You fought for me and won.
Today, let my voice join yours, singing songs of delight.

Lord, you are the one who sees beyond all my shortcomings and takes joy in me.
Help me not despise the work you are doing in my life.
Help me love you with a pure and grateful heart. Amen.

Watch over your heart with all diligence,
for from it flow the springs of life.
Proverbs 4:23 (NASB)

THE SPRINGS OF LIFE

You hypocrites! Well did Isaiah prophesy of you, when he said:
"This people honors me with their lips,
But their heart is far from me; in vain do they worship me,
teaching as doctrines the commandments of men."
Matthew 15:7–9 (ESV)

Today, you must put hypocrisy far from you.

Let me tell you why I hate it: there is more horror in a dead thing that acts alive than a dead thing that lies buried.

What does this mean for me?

There is more wickedness in a sinner who acts righteous than one who shows what they truly are.

What do I do?

Reject, today, all empty motions of spirituality, all false appearances of worship. Examine your heart with care, for the springs of life are in it, and if that water turns to bitter poison it will harm many who are thirsty.

Forgive me.

I have. That is why I tell you to guard your heart. Teach the truth. Forsake appearances. If you are dead inside, tell me. I will make you alive. But if you exalt yourself as a hypocrite? I promise you this: I will teach you humility.

And that lesson may not be gentle.

Holy Father, forgive me for the hypocrisy in my life.
Help me to surrender all to you—the falseness I hide and the falseness
to which I am blind. Let me be holy, caring more to live truly as
your child than to appear righteous. Let my heart please you. Amen.

What more should I say?... Others suffered mocking and flogging, and even
chains and imprisonment. They were stoned to death, they were sawn in two, they
were killed by the sword; they went about in skins of sheep and goats, destitute,
persecuted, tormented—of whom the world was not worthy.
Hebrews 11:32, 36–37 (NRSV)

THE HARDEST KIND OF GOOD

Blessed are those who are persecuted for righteousness' sake,
for theirs is the kingdom of heaven.
Matthew 5:10 (NRSV)

ﻮﻟ

Blood has a voice. When Cain slew his brother, painting humanity's sunrise the color of death, it cried to me from the ground. I marked the murderer with mercy, but I did not silence the blood. It wails from under my own throne, from the foundations of my holy house. The red pools of history wait for justice.

It is too much. Why do you not protect your own?

[silence]

Are you so uncaring? Are you so weak?

[silence]

What good could the torment of your children bring? Are you so cruel?

Oh, child—the story is not ended yet. You could not ask such things if your heart was not made in my image. You would not feel them unless you belonged in my kingdom. You would care nothing for justice if I was unjust. I am the avenger of blood, the trampler of death, the one who suffers with you all. I am perfect in grace, perfect in justice. The one who hears. The one who knows. There is no wrong that will not be broken into rightness. And though I will not answer your questions now, I will ask you one in return: Child of Adam, what evil has there ever been in the history of the bloodied sky that is too great for me to turn to the fiercest, the deepest kind of good?

ﻮﻟ

Lord, it is hard to understand your ways and your timing.
Help me trust that you are good and that all evil may be one day redeemed
for your purposes. Bless all who suffer for your sake. Amen.

I will seek the lost, and I will bring back the strayed.
Ezekiel 34:16 (ESV)

THE SEEKING

The hour is coming, and is now here, when the true worshipers will worship the Father in spirit and truth, for the Father is seeking such people to worship him.
John 4:23 (ESV)

Give to the one who seeks you the gift of love,
for he loves you.
How far I have come to care for you,
like a shepherd, because my flock had been sent running.

Lord, I praise you from my heart.

I sought you.
Now seek me.
I called you back by name.
Now, will you call upon mine?
I adored you and gave myself to you and loved you above any treasure.
The kingdom of heaven is like a man who counted all things as nothing
except the thing he loved.
Mine is that kingdom, and it must be yours
for you to live in my love.

You are beyond my praise.

But how I still long to hear you!
Will your seeking heart learn
to lift songs with me?
Finding me is joy indeed,
as was finding you.

Lord, you have searched for every one of us. Thank you for your kind pursuit and the limitless humility and kindness of your heart. Help me to praise you, as a sign and seal of my love, and a gift of gratitude for yours. Amen.

O LORD, you hear the desire of the afflicted;
you will strengthen their heart.
Psalm 10:17 (ESV)

STRONG-HEARTED

You will incline your ear to do justice to the fatherless and the oppressed,
so that man who is of the earth may strike terror no more.
Psalm 10:17–18 (ESV)

I see today. I see every day. I see all joy. All bloodshed. I see all virtue, all wickedness, all freedom, all oppression.

Deliver us from evil.

I hear today. I hear every day. Every laugh. Every scream. Every parent grieving their child. Every cry of pain or fear. Every happy sigh. Every anguished moan.

How can you bear it all?

My heart is strong. Today, hear this one thing: the one who sees all will make all right. There is no injustice I will not correct. There is no loss I will not restore. There is no bloodshed I will not avenge. There is no cry I will not answer. There is no weak one I will not save.

Today, join your heart to mine. Allow yourself to feel the throbbing pain of the world. Today, hope in me. Today, lift your voice in prayer. Name the needy. Tell me their suffering. And then know well, child of man, how short the time is before I roar like a raging wave over the sandcastles of violence and oppression, covering the earth with my justice like the water covers the sea.

King of all, you are the source of all rightness and justice.
You have promised to care for the oppressed and the suffering.
You have promised to wipe away every tear. Let your strong-hearted justice
and mercy come quickly, and make me and all your people agents of your
righteousness for the service of the world and the glory of Jesus. Amen.

He humbled you, causing you to hunger and then feeding you . . .
to teach you that man does not live on bread alone
but on every word that comes from the mouth of the LORD.
Deuteronomy 8:3 (NIV)

A WORD FOR THE EATER

As the rain and the snow come down from heaven,
and do not return there until they have watered the earth, making it
bring forth and sprout, giving seed to the sower and bread to the eater,
so shall my word be that goes out from my mouth; it shall not return to me empty.
Isaiah 55:10–11 (NRSV)

Every need you have is a gift.

How is that?

Hunger points you to me, the one who feeds. Cold pushes you to me, the one who clothes. Every longing and lack is meant to be met by provision from my hand—in my way, in my timing, for your good. You long for truth, for you are made in the image of the True.

At least, that is how it should be. But you seem to only want what makes you comfortable, what pleases your ears and confirms your opinions. You gorge yourself on what you like of what I say, but turn your nose up the moment I put before you the nourishing thing you need but do not want. Manna is better than meat in the wilderness; the body of Christ much better than the flesh of fowls. So why do you complain at the table I lay in the desert?

Forgive me.

My word will not return to me without benefit, without life, without nourishing all who call me Father. I will feed you, just as I water my fields that lay full of the sprouting seeds, raising the bread of God. You will be given bread and body. You will become bread and body.

I will give you all you need. Whether it is what you want? That's up to you.

Lord, your provision is perfect and your word is sure.
Help me to humbly turn to you for all I need. Amen.

Come, behold the works of the LORD;
see what desolations he has brought on the earth.
He makes wars cease to the end of the earth;
he breaks the bow, and shatters the spear;
he burns the shields with fire.
Psalm 46:8–9 (NRSV)

THE WARBREAKER

They shall beat their swords into plowshares,
and their spears into pruning hooks;
nation shall not lift up sword against nation,
neither shall they learn war any more.
Isaiah 2:4 (NRSV)

ﻌﯾ

For now, it is enough to say this: I have already risen
to bring battle to Battle, to war against War,
to bend the joints of Bloodshed backwards until they roll apart.
I will slay Slaying, and Death will die with my foot on his neck.

But you are a God of peace.

Ah! Do not mistake me for cruel,
but neither mistake me for gentle on the day I buckle armor on my
children.
Who knew that I would muster the weak and make them unopposable?
Prepare for war like this:
with love even for your enemy,
and remembering the prophecy that the prisoners of evil whisper in hope—
"Even now, God paints his children for war
and tells his servants that, before evening, enemies will kneel for mercy."
My Word is a blade. To lay hearts open, to separate bone and marrow.
To kill. And to make alive.
My peace defends the weak.

ﻌﯾ

Lord, you are mighty and good. In Jesus you have begun the final battle against evil.
Let me be peaceable and brave, awaiting your deliverance and working
for the way of Jesus, which will overthrow all violence. Amen.

I made a covenant with my eyes not to look lustfully. . . .
Does he not see my ways and count my every step?
Job 31:1, 4 (NIV)

CONCEPTION

Each person is tempted when they are dragged away by their own
evil desire and enticed. Then, after desire has conceived, it gives birth to sin;
and sin, when it is full-grown, gives birth to death.
James 1:14–15 (NIV)

I watch as you awake from a night of sleep. Did you dream enough? I suppose not. The morning is bright, but you do not see it. Your mind is turned the wrong way. You face the wrong things.

Desire drags you like a stallion foaming for his mare. You fight it for a moment, but your heart is not in it. Your desire has already conceived, and every womb must empty.

Death will come of it, in the end.

What then? Help me.

Ask the question.

What question?

You know. The question you most fear. In all the desire, all the distraction, all the destruction and all the dead promises, tell me one thing: who are you searching for?

Father, you know me better than I know myself. You know the pull of sin
on me—how I am torn between what I crave and what you say is good
for my heart. Please give me strength to surrender all of myself to you—
every thought, every choice, every desire. May I be wholly yours. Amen.

God spoke to our ancestors in many and various ways by the prophets, but
in these last days he has spoken to us by a Son, whom he appointed heir of all things.
Hebrews 1:1–2 (NRSV)

HEIRS

If we are children, then we are heirs—heirs of God and co-heirs with Christ,
if indeed we share in his sufferings in order that we may also share in his glory.
Romans 8:17 (NIV)

All the kings and captains of the earth will be buried in it.
The powers that think themselves above you shuffle,
single file,
to sleep with the dead and suffer nightmares of a resurrection in which
the last is first.
They dread my Anointed.

>   *Come quickly, Lord Jesus.*

Let this comfort you:
on the funeral day, when vaults are opened to receive, though
Death thinks himself a prince,
I will bury him.

>   *You almost make me weep with hope.*

One day, this will all be yours.
Life will sprout.
You will rule with the Son.
What is mine is his,
and what is his is yours.
Kiss him.
For the earth will belong to the meek,
and my gentle children shall
ride wolves
to the final battle.

>   *Lord, thank you for being perfect in mercy and perfect in justice.*
>   *Thank you for adopting me as your true child and heir in Jesus.*
>   *Let me live with the humble authority of your Son. Amen.*

The LORD is my chosen portion. . . .
indeed, I have a beautiful inheritance.
Psalm 16:5–6 (ESV)

DESIRING DELIGHT

Delight yourself in the LORD
and he will give you the desires of your heart.
Psalm 37:4 (ESV)

⁓

Today, let us share joy. How wonderful it is to live as one. My wholeness brings delight, and my kindness overflows all around you. My Spirit is close and waiting to speak goodness to you.

I long for it, Father!

Then take joy in me. Joy, right now, in this moment—in this hour, this day, this season, this year. This lifetime. Take joy and delight! Because here is the secret: delight shapes your heart. If I make you glad, your gladness is unshakeable, and you begin to be unshakeable. In me, your joy is well placed. It is beyond the reach of danger or circumstance. Let this day bring what it may, for in me delight is rooted more deeply than any trial.

You are so good.

Yes, and better still than you know. Now, what do you desire?

You.

Then I will be yours.

⁓

Father, help me find my deepest gladness in you.
Let me desire your love, desire to know you fully,
beyond any other longing in my life. Amen.

Jesus said to him, "Have you believed because you have seen me?
Blessed are those who have not seen and yet have come to believe."
John 20:29 (NRSV)

THE BLESSED UNSEEN

Although you have not seen him, you love him.
1 Peter 1:8 (NRSV)

_᳴

Today, faith stirs in your heart, deeper than you recognize.

You notice your doubts, mostly. They are all you can see sometimes. But I hardly notice them at all. What I see is the hidden jewel of faith—like a diamond on the floor of an unlit room, unnoticed, until morning comes, when it splinters the sun into more colors than your eye can see. Faith in the dark need only wait for dawn.

I want to believe, but it is so hard sometimes.

There are those who have seen God in Jesus Christ, who have walked with him, eaten fresh fish he cooked over a fire made of driftwood. There are those who drank water he drew up for them, those who ate bread he broke, those who worked beside him, wept with him, laid their head on his breast to hear his heart. They saw miracles, signs that made the leap of faith very short.

You have not seen, so doubt is not the mystery. Faith is. You live by it now. You are blessed by it.

Even so, Lord, help my unbelief.

Let me refine and purify you. Let me, whom you have not seen, draw you nearer. Take one step toward me—I will come the rest of the way and bless you as I come, with the joy of glory that is beyond any telling of it.

You often ask to see me. Ask instead for me to let you see your heart as I see it. I will do it. Look! The glimmer within, beautiful and stark, is proof that you are blessed already.

_᳴

Father, you are worthy of all my faith and confidence.
But it is not easy for me. Please give me the strength to turn
to you with my whole self, and help me see my heart as you see it. Amen.

It is in vain that you rise up early and go late to rest,
eating the bread of anxious toil; for he gives sleep to his beloved.
Psalm 127:2 (NRSV)

TO SLEEP SECURE

The fear of the LORD is life indeed;
filled with it one rests secure and suffers no harm.
Proverbs 19:23 (NRSV)

In the hours of the night,
when shadows stalk,
do you sleep in faith,
or lie uneasy in the arms of worry?

Too little of the first and too much of the second, to tell you the truth.

Why do you not trust me?
The one who rules the day rules the night as well.
The one who renews the soul renews your mind and body
in sleep,
in rest,
in the hours of the night.

Fear me alone, and all other fears will die.
Embrace holy fear,
which is nothing else than faith,
nothing else than reverence,
nothing else than worship,
than peace, than rest,
than the security of perfect love,
which guards you from darkness all the hours of the night.

Fear me, little dreamer, and all other fears will die like shadows in the light.

Lord, you are the God of perfect rest. Help my faith in you grow until
my soul, body, and mind are all united in trust, and I am able to release fear.
Help me relax and rest under your care. Amen.

Where can I go from your Spirit? Where can I flee from your presence?
If I go up to the heavens, you are there;
if I make my bed in the depths, you are there.
If I rise on the wings of the dawn, if I settle on the far side of the sea,
even there your hand will guide me, your right hand will hold me fast.
Psalm 139:7–10 (NIV)

EVEN HERE

Then Jacob woke from his sleep and said,
"Surely the LORD is in this place—and I did not know it!"
Genesis 28:16 (NRSV)

Where are you, Father?

Here.

Why do you hide from me?

I have always been here. It is you who hid and cannot find the way back.

Why do you make me search?

You would not care much for the finding if the search was easy. It is the work of a growing heart to ask, to knock, to seek. There is no place I am not, no time that is not mine. If I chose to tear the veil, you would see the truth—your Maker is behind all that is made. The rock that is your pillow is the threshold of heaven. The stars are a clock wound for you, for all the generations of the earth. The ticking of the constellations is a sign of my faithfulness.

My presence is perfect. In your moments of deepest loneliness, I held you. You thought you dreamt in a barren desert that night, yet you were lying at the doorway to my house, guarded by the stewards of the door and fed by my own hand. Look around you. I have been in this place from before the beginning of beginnings.

Surely, I am in every place. But do you believe it?

Lord, your Spirit is in all places and all times.
Let my faith grow until I see you clearly in my life. Amen.

If one member suffers, all suffer together with it; if one member is honored,
all rejoice together with it. Now you are the body of Christ
and individually members of it.

1 Corinthians 12:26–27 (NRSV)

ALL AND EVERYONE

Bear one another's burdens, and in this way you will fulfill the law of Christ.

Galatians 6:2 (NRSV)

ﮗ

Into the sanctuary, Christ the Priest leads a procession of joy.
Laughter and fellowship are not irreverent to the God of all happiness,
so let there be songs of merriment
as well as prayers and the curling blue smoke of incense.
Let the children approach with their elders
to cling to the altar and hear the story of the seven-eyed Lamb
who was laid on these stones by his own Father
and how, in that moment of sacrifice,
the whole madcap world became a thicket
in which God caught himself by the horns.
There is room for all in the holy of holies.
Come in closer! Enter and be one!

Lord, let me draw near with the rest.

Here, nothing shall be lacking.
Who is weak among you? Let that one lean on another.
Who is rich? Let that one settle another's accounts.
May the one with little to carry help the one with much,
and let the one with great faith carry the doubter.
Lift holy hands! Let the ancient doors witness the dawn,
the spring,
the new youth of the world
on the faces of all and everyone.

ﮗ

Lord, you have called all your people into unity in Jesus and baptized us
into the same Spirit. Let us all live as one, bearing one another's burdens
and sharing one another's joys as Christ himself does for us. Amen.

I led them with cords of kindness, with the bands of love,
and I became to them as one who eases the yoke on their jaws,
and I bent down to them and fed them.

Hosea 11:4 (ESV)

THE CORDS OF KINDNESS

Do you not realize that God's kindness
is meant to lead you to repentance?

Romans 2:4 (NRSV)

You were once chained to death—a blind slave lashed to the millstone, treading an endless circle of dead days.

You ground out sin and were paid in slow death. How your withered muscles ached, chafed by hemp and iron. The sun passed over, but you did not see it, and all you heard was the mockery of a false master.

I set you free. I required no key but my will, and no sword but my word. Your strong master was bound and cast into the ruins of his divided house.

Praise you for it, Lord.

I freed you and dressed you and bound your wounds. I gave you back your sight. I placed on you the gentlest and most pleasant of bonds: kindness and love.

Your kindness has never felt like bondage.

Then why do you pull against the cords?

Beloved, what will it take, after these many days, for you to turn your heart and be present at my table without thinking fondly of the bitter husks flung to you in your misery by the laughing enemy?

Lord, you have set me free from all other masters and led me in your kindness
and love. Still, I confess that my heart is often turned toward myself, the world,
and the evil rulers of this age. Please help me repent of all my sin
and cling to you as my true and perfect master. Amen.

He will cover you with his pinions, and under his wings you will find refuge;
his faithfulness is a shield and buckler.
Psalm 91:4 (NRSV)

THE FEATHERS OF GOD

How often I have longed to gather your children together,
as a hen gathers her chicks under her wings, and you were not willing.
Matthew 23:37 (NIV)

ـهيو

The arrows hiss like snakes, seeking that place between your shoulders. Snares lie hidden in the long grass, hungry for your feet. There is terror by noon in this world, illness by night. I see you recoil from what snarls in the dark, startled by what watches from the moonless trees.

> *I am afraid.*

Hunted ones are right to fear. For all its goodness, this life is never safe.

There are many who have been lost in the dark, many wandering still. I call to them, for I have not lost one of those who came to me. My wings spread wide enough for all the weak and wounded. One day, they will cover the world again in my shadow, which is the light.

> *Cover me now, Lord.*

Yes! Draw near, and I will draw near to you. Tell me your troubles. Whisper up your prayers through my feathers. What fool would dare reach for you? I would wither him. I would show him mercy of the harshest kind—breaking the teeth he'd have torn you with, feathering him with my own arrows, catching the trapper in the slicing noose of his own snare.

This is my eternal promise: to be your protector, your refuge from every danger, the one who hides you, who guides you, who comforts you and all those who come to me. Nothing could hurt you here, for my wings are stone and my chest a soft down upon which to lay your head.

But are you willing to be sheltered?

ـهيو

Lord, you are the protector of the weak and oppressed, a friend to every one
of us who has need of your shelter. Please help me accept your refuge. Amen.

For the LORD takes pleasure in his people;
he adorns the humble with victory.
Psalm 149:4 (NRSV)

A VICTORIOUS FASHION

As God's chosen ones, holy and beloved, clothe yourselves
with compassion, kindness, humility, meekness, and patience.
Colossians 3:12 (NRSV)

‿ورﻟ

Let me dress you in the gracious way,
with the kindness of your oldest friend,
the elegance of perfection.
No clothier can rival my skill with thread and needle,
the fashion of a future that has not yet come to your race—
dignified, weathered by eternity.
Victory is beautiful, colored like hope, with the strength of kindness.
Put it on.

I wish to live as you do, God.

Here, then. The fit was tailored to you. The cut is bold.
Sewn into the hem is a blessing of protection:

DO NOT FEAR THE TERROR THAT HUNTS BY NIGHT
NOR THE ARROW THAT SLAYS BY NOON LIGHT
NOR THE SICKNESS IN DREAD DARK
NOR THE PLAGUE IN HIGH SUN

Embroidered on the collar: a wheat stalk, a lamp wick, a two-edged
    sword, a pouring cup.
A true garment this is, made for the gleaners of fields,
for the lamp-lit women waiting for the wedding feast,
for the wilds of the battled valley, for the guests of the evening party.
Perfection! On you, my child, victory is the perfect fit.

Father. Thank you.

‿ورﻟ

Lord, you have given me victory, salvation, and the joy of your Spirit.
Help me turn fully toward you, to live and embrace every good thing.
Help me put on the virtues you have given me to wear. Amen.

Heal me, O Lord, and I shall be healed;
save me, and I shall be saved; for you are my praise.
Jeremiah 17:14 (NRSV)

THE HEALER

Surely he has borne our infirmities and carried our diseases;
yet we accounted him stricken, struck down by God, and afflicted.
But he was wounded for our transgressions, crushed for our iniquities; upon him
was the punishment that made us whole, and by his bruises we are healed.
Isaiah 53:4–5 (NRSV)

You cry for healing, and the world pulls back, afraid of infection. But only the sickly fear sickness, and only the mortal fears death. I hear you, and I answer.

Then I will be healed?

Yes, but never the way you expect.

Look! Here comes my Son, the Healer. He is me, yet not me. He is perfect health, yet covered in utter sickness. Righteousness inviolable, turned scapegoat, the lamb of weakness.

See his bruises flower. Kiss him. Weep with him. Lay your hands on his hair and feel your sickness go into him, his life enter your dead bones.

See the Stricken One stagger. See him crushed under the bloody world, limbs bent ways limbs should not go. The Blessed One is cursed, hung like hospital rags on a tree. I am the present Father—holding, strengthening, providing, helping him drink the whole of our bitter cup. I let the spear find his heart, my own breaks yet leaps.

The deathless does not fear death. Only strength unthinkable can become perfect in weakness.

I cannot understand.

Then receive.

Father, you are all perfection and all life. Help me live the life
of Jesus in depth and truth, allowing him to give me his perfect life. Amen.

Righteous Father, though the world does not know you, I know you,
and they know that you have sent me. I have made you known to them,
and will continue to make you known in order that the love you have for me
may be in them and that I myself may be in them.
John 17:25–26 (NIV)

KNOWN

We destroy arguments and every lofty opinion raised against
the knowledge of God, and take every thought captive to obey Christ.
2 Corinthians 10:5 (ESV)

Lord, I want to know you.

What do those words mean?

silence

You want to know me? Look to the earth and sea, the glistening galaxies, the law of life that is graven on your heart.

I AM.

See my sign carved in the bowing trees, hear my name pulse beneath the city streets, see my face, for a moment, in the eyes of a child.

silence

You want to know me? Read my book, the strange and treasured labors of many pens. Consume it like food or medicine. It is sweet and bitter—that is how life tastes to the newly born.

You really want to know me? Look to Jesus. He is the imprint of my nature stamped into human clay. He is love absolute, the king and conqueror clothed as the least of the house servants. Follow him, rejoice with him, mourn with him. Dig your grave with him, and die with him, and let me raise you.

Lord, I want to know you and be known by you.

Then come and live.

Lord, you are worthy of all devotion and love. Help me know you not for who I
want you to be, or according to any false idea, but for who you truly are. Amen.

RIGHT

I know, O LORD, that your judgments are right,
and that in faithfulness you have humbled me.
Psalm 119:75 (NRSV)

In the dark of night, a prophet once whispered, "Heed the rod, and the One who appointed it." Do you think his words are empty? Can you not hear their wisdom? I speak and tug and prompt and pull. Yet you walk toward death.

It seems cruel of you to punish your children.

That is folly, and you know it.

Love is limiting. It breaks walls between and builds walls around. It is the teeth of the mother wolf that teaches her cubs the way of life. She nips them, that their enemy may not rend them. She barks, that the shadows may not devour. She tosses them by the back of their stiff necks, that their precious bones, hearing the howl of her wisdom, may not be ground by bloody jaws.

Like a father loves his lost son, like the beloved waits in agony outside the locked door, I love you. I love you with tenderness and fury. I love you with a rich table to nourish you—and a rod to guide.

Chasten me if you must, until I have no choice but to obey.
Though I only half believe it, only your way can be life.

Lord, your way is right and perfect. But it is hard to understand and harder yet to do. Have mercy on me. Help me out of my foolishness and weakness. May your discipline be as gentle as your rich love will allow. Let me be an eager learner and a beloved child. Amen.

Simon Peter answered, "You are the Messiah, the Son of the living God."
And Jesus answered him, "Blessed are you, Simon son of Jonah!
For flesh and blood has not revealed this to you, but my Father in heaven."
Matthew 16:16–17 (NRSV)

REVEALED

I want you to understand that no one speaking by
the Spirit of God ever says "Let Jesus be cursed!"
and no one can say "Jesus is Lord" except by the Holy Spirit.
1 Corinthians 12:3 (NRSV)

Whose is the breath that fills your lungs?

It is yours.

You take from it, shape it with your tongue, and form it into a word. It enters the world, like steam on a cold day, to enter the heart of your hearers.

Whose is the Spirit that fills your heart?

Yours too, Father.

Yes, mine, for the Spirit is me.

In me, you shape the truth of the world according to some measure of your own shape. In my Spirit you speak echoes of the one Word that has been from the beginning.

Not one of my words has ever fallen to the ground. When you are speechless, let me be your perfect speech. When you have no truth left, speak, and my truth will be enough for the both of us. We will prophesy, we will encourage, we will comfort, and we will sing.

Could it be that I am at times your tongue?

Yes, and it pleases me.
Speak well, by my Spirit.

Father, all your words are truth. Please let me know and speak your truth
in a world filled with deceit. Let me breathe your wisdom.
Fill me with your perfect Spirit, and grant me boldness in him. Amen.

Those who turn away from you shall be written in the earth,
for they have forsaken the LORD, the fountain of living water.
Jeremiah 17:13 (ESV)

THE WATER FORSAKEN

Jesus bent down and wrote with his finger on the ground.
And as they continued to ask him, he stood up and said to them,
"Let him who is without sin among you be the first to throw a stone at her."
John 8:6–7 (ESV)

Why have you forsaken me, child?

When have I ever forsaken you?

You answer that.
Do you understand what repentance is?
Repentance is turning from your death to my life.
Repentance is turning from your guilt to my mercy.
Repentance is turning from your own name,
written in the dust of death,
to my fountain of water that lives.

I have repented. I am righteous.

Then what is that stone in your hand?
And why do you imagine the sound it will make
when it strikes the head of another sinner?
And why, do you think,
if you are so righteous,
that you are still so thirsty?

Lord, only you are perfect in righteousness. I confess my own pride
and self-righteousness and repent of everything I do to elevate myself
in judgment above others, knowing that in so doing I separate
myself from you. Help me turn always to your Spirit. Amen.

My child, if sinners entice you, do not consent.
Proverbs 1:10 (NRSV)

THE BLESSED NO

Happy are those who do not follow the advice of the wicked,
or take the path that sinners tread, or sit in the seat of scoffers;
but their delight is in the law of the LORD,
and on his law they meditate day and night.
Psalm 1:1–2 (NRSV)

There is a broad road that leads to death. Many are those who find it.

It is pleasant at first, and easy to enter. There are many who steer others into it, calling them to join. It is effortless to go along. It is a good time, mostly, at the start. There is laughing and talk of common sense. "This is how life should be," they say with an attractive sense of worldly wisdom. There are rewards, too, but they are empty. Not because of what they are, but because of where they are—on the road that leads away from me.

I am afraid. I am easily tempted.

Yes, but not as easily as you think. There is more strength in you than you know. And you will need it.

Many will try to lure you down the road of death. They will offer you things you want, say words you want to hear. It will seem like the most sensible thing in the world to walk away from me. But you always have a choice, though it may not seem that way. There is always escape.

In such a moment, help me be strong.

I have. I am. I will. Life is close to all, but anyone can be tempted to walk away from it, hand in hand with the friends who are not friends. You will know them by their fruit.

Speak to them the blessed "no." And walk into life, into my perfect "yes."

Lord, you are holy and wise. In my world filled with temptations
and distractions, let me know the good from the evil and walk
in your ways in the holiness and true love of Jesus Christ. Amen.

Let us know, let us press on to know the LORD;
his appearing is as sure as the dawn; he will come to us like the showers,
like the spring rains that water the earth.

Hosea 6:3 (NRSV)

PRESSING ON

I press on toward the goal for the prize of
the heavenly call of God in Christ Jesus.

Philippians 3:14 (NRSV)

ﭳ

Simple things are the hardest to do. Today, lift up those weak hands. How far you have come already! I know how hard it is. You are doing well.

I want to know you.

And every day you are. You push to know me more, through the world of things that are easily seen, through the struggles with your enemy, through the tired difficulties of your work and waiting. You push, you press. You grow. You are strengthened.

I give you what you need to finish in power. I give you what you need to believe. I who call you am faithful, like the unfailing sun that warms the globe or the rainy season that wakens roots beneath the earth.

Recognize, in the deepest place of your soul, the knowledge of this truth— though life has been hard, I have strengthened you to overcome it. I have provided, have grounded, have upheld. I have brightened the road with joy. I have planted good things with grace. I have called up the sprouts of faith with wisdom.

I have seen, and I believe. Help me press on.

I will. Now, while you are still on the dark road, with the harsh wind in your face and the dust whispering about your feet. Now and long after the dawn of heaven has brightened the world into unending day.

ﭳ

Lord, you are faithful and good. You know the strain of pursuit, of drawing
near, of pushing through the difficulties of life. Help me to know you right
where I am today—but to also press on in faithfulness toward the call of Jesus,
that I may know and love you better every day of my life. Amen.

NEARER

Let your gentleness be known to everyone. The Lord is near.
Philippians 4:5 (NRSV)

To me, all places are "here."
To me, all times are "now."
All wisdom calls me Teacher;
all the worlds call me their Source.

And yet, I come nearer.
Though I have always been in every place,
I come nearer by your invitation, nearer by your gentle holiness.
Righteousness summons me, who cannot be commanded by any word
of power.
Holiness beckons me, the one none can compel.

Open your arms, and I will hold you tighter.
Do not be of a divided heart.
Say "come" and find me anew.
That finding will be life,
and love,
and gentleness.

> *Come.*

Father, you desire to know me and be known by me.
Let me open my heart and mind, so you can be with me intimately
and with all the good gentleness of your presence. Amen.

Let the heavens be glad, and let the earth rejoice;
let the sea roar, and all that fills it; let the field exult,
and everything in it. Then shall all the trees of the forest sing for joy
before the LORD; for he is coming, for he is coming to judge the earth.
Psalm 96:11–13 (NRSV)

THE JOYOUS JUDGE

For the time has come for judgment to begin with the household of God.
1 Peter 4:17 (NRSV)

⁓

There are things creation knows that man has long forgotten.

Justice is in the elements I made—the very rocks and water remember that there is one who judges justly, who made all things in their season. I am the Watcher, eyes in every place. From me no secrets are hidden. To me all must give account, from the eldest star to the freshest newborn. My rulings are perfect in beauty—all rightness and balance reside in my decrees. I hate nothing I have made.

Praise to you.

All who fear my judgments fear only for themselves. Creation does not fear, but rejoices. The oppressed do not fear to hear that I am keeping account. They praise me, call upon me, crying, "Come quickly!" Perfect love casts out fear, and those who know that all my judgments are love are unafraid. They rejoice.

In the bent grass, the falling rain, the fertile fields, the thrum of cities: anticipation. Your own cells cherish the truth you often fear: I come to judge. At that reminder, all good things rejoice.

Is my judgment good news to you?

I begin in my own household, calling my children and stewards to report. Rightness begins with us. Peace and mercy begin with us. Justice and good reward begin with us. And so, with us, begins the rejoicing!

⁓

Lord, you are perfect in all that you do and decide. In your presence, no wicked
thing or deed can stand. Make me holy, that I, too, might anticipate
your judgment and fully rejoice in all your good restoration. Amen.

No one who puts his hand to the plow and looks back is fit for the kingdom of God.
Luke 9:62 (ESV)

THE LINES OF THE PLOW

Having begun by the Spirit, are you now being perfected by the flesh?
Galatians 3:3 (ESV)

~ه

God, I am bad at this. Crooked.

A furrow is not made straight by the hands of the plowman,
but by his eyes.
If you look behind, to the side,
or to your feet which walk the fallow field,
your line will writhe in the earth, crooked as a fox's hind leg.
Instead, look where you are going—
that tree planted by the far stream, perhaps,
or my tower, hedged among the vineyards.
Look to the finish, and walk forward.

Help me?

I am.
I know your doubts, your pride.
I also know your passion; you long for my kingdom.
I know your love.

But every step is a chance to stray. Give me some rules.

Do not be a fool, even a good-hearted one.
Do not turn your eye, or your heart will follow.
Do not look for a new law.
Do not kill through "good behavior"
what I am planting in the Spirit.
Look, and walk, and let me make alive
in this field of good and holy danger.

~ه

*Lord, help me not turn to any distraction that might keep me
from continuing life in your Spirit, especially any
perceived righteousness not given to me by Jesus. Amen.*

Beware of practicing your piety before others in order to be seen by them.
Matthew 6:1–2 (NRSV)

THE PRACTICE OF PLEASING

Am I now seeking human approval, or God's approval? Or am I trying
to please people? If I were still pleasing people, I would not be a servant of Christ.
Galatians 1:10 (NRSV)

‿ِܦ

Don't say you don't love it: the applause, the warm hand on the back, the affirmation. The acceptance.

I do love it.

What would you not do for approval? You would change yourself, wear a different face. How far would you take it? Would you even deny me, if it came to it, so as not to be mocked away from the fire at twilight?

Please, don't let that be true.

You tell me what is true.

No man can serve two masters. Wisdom is jeered wherever she walks. "Follow me," Jesus said. And look where his path led. They cast him out of every respectable establishment. Even his brothers rebuked him. The leaders sought to kill him and eventually succeeded. His hosts were whores and money launderers. How pleasing to the people that was!

His hair grew like his cousin's in the desert. The birds and foxes were wealthier than he who governs the world. Charity fed him. He depended on hospitality for roof after roof over his head. He was loved by few, hated by many. He was welcomed by the poor, rejected by the rich. He turned blessing upside down, honoring the lowly with his quiet presence.

See with the Lord's eye today. Lust for no approval. Serve and follow. The streets may empty before you, and doors may be closed.

Tell me: what will you seek today?

‿ِܦ

Lord, you are the only one whose opinion of me matters. But still I confess
that I desire approval from other people, looking to them for affirmation of
who I am. Help me never change myself to please any besides you. Amen.

Now his elder son was in the field; and when he came and approached
the house, he heard music and dancing. He called one of the slaves and asked
what was going on. He replied, "Your brother has come."
Luke 15:25–27 (NRSV)

THE ELDER ONE

Enter His gates with thanksgiving and His courts with praise.
Psalm 100:4 (HCSB)

In the story of the prodigal, there were two sons: younger and elder. The younger wished death to the father by asking for his inheritance early, then spent a fortune on booze and fast company.

The elder did all the father ever asked. He tended stony fields, sweated under the hot sun. He put off seeing his friends until after the harvest was in and the sheaves were bundled in rows, long and neat.

I remember the story.

So which son are you? Perhaps you are the younger, the rule-breaker, the wastrel child who frittered the gifts of heaven away on the pleasures of death. Perhaps chasing the wind broke you, and you slunk home, whimpering. Perhaps your Father met you in the road and rejoiced, for the dead thing was alive.

But perhaps you are the one who does everything right. Perhaps you are the self-righteous rule-keeper, the sullen good kid. Perhaps you died but did not feel it. Perhaps you are the lonely one who stands outside my party with folded arms, refusing the feast because it nourishes an undeserving belly. Perhaps you have never tasted your inheritance because mercy makes you bitter. Perhaps you need my compassion as much as any prodigal. Perhaps you need it more.

Come in, child. Enter the house. Join the presence, and praise.
It looks cold where you are standing.

Lord, your mercy goes deeper than fairness.
Help me embrace your kindness and enter your joy. Amen.

I will save the lame
and gather the outcast,
and I will change their shame into praise
and renown in all the earth.

Zephaniah 3:19 (ESV)

THE RENOWN OF THE LAME

But Peter said, "I have no silver or gold, but what I have I give you;
in the name of Jesus Christ of Nazareth, stand up and walk."

Acts 3:6 (NRSV)

ﻭ

You who sit or stumble,
whose feet are wrenched backwards,
leaving monstrous footprints,
you who beg for scraps from anyone with a look of mercy,
hear me.

I'm listening.

Nothing you see will remain the same. The day is breaking, and with it breaks the ancient curse, the shadow of your people. It turns to blessing. The withered hands are lifted up—the joy of youth flowing back through the marrow of warped bones. Healing is in my hands, and they are stretched to you. I love you. I will be gentle. I will heal.

Blessed is the name of my Son, who carried all your wounds and gave you all his wholeness! Rejoice, lame one. Rejoice. Your hope is not wasted, for every promise of mine will stand.

And so will you.

ﻭ

Father, you are the great healer of all things. You know what needs
healing and have promised to make all of me whole—body, soul, and mind—
in your time. Please grant me your perfect healing and the patience to wait
for your full redemption to come to this hurting world. Amen.

*I consider that our present sufferings are not worth
comparing with the glory that will be revealed in us.*
Romans 8:18 (NIV)

THE TIME BETWEEN

*Wait for the LORD;
be strong, and let your heart take courage;
wait for the LORD!*
Psalm 27:14 (ESV)

You feel
exhausted.
I know.
But I am coming like the dawn,
like the bitter light in the eyes of sleepers
that will be sweet when day has blossomed.

     Help me.

By my Spirit, you will be strong enough to overcome.
Wait for me,
my child,
and you will see wonders.

*Lord, you have promised that you will bring restoration to all things.
Please let me be faithful as I wait for you.
Let me know and proclaim your goodness. Amen.*

Do not worry about anything, but in everything by prayer and
supplication with thanksgiving let your requests be made known to God.
And the peace of God, which surpasses all understanding,
will guard your hearts and your minds in Christ Jesus.
Philippians 4:6–7 (NRSV)

THE BONFIRE OF WORRY

Cast all your anxiety on him, because he cares for you.
1 Peter 5:7 (NRSV)

I am here.

Listen! Do you hear the anger of the world, swirling like wind in the thorn tree? Do you hear the hiss of its cruelty? Do you feel the sting and spit of it, seeking to terrify, to distract, to kill?

Yes, and I am angry at my fear.

It has no power.

Let me tell you a story of your future:

There is a brush pile I have made, in a field beside a river. On it I have heaped the cares of all my children. The worry is all broken out—its stalks snapped, its poison dry. It is only brushwood now, thorns and weedy thistles. One word from me will spark a blaze.

Burn!

Yes. And you shall dance there with me, leaping the fire and laughing. All my children will spit in the ash of dead worries. We will paint our faces with them and laugh in our holy wildness. We will watch the embers glow until, deep in the pile, we see the glint of gold and silver—treasure long hidden by the brush. We will pull it out and drape ourselves with beauty, white-hot and pure. We will laugh at the white flames, until the stars look down and say, "Tonight, a sister has been born to us." And so bright our joy will be, flashing like rubies, that their words will be true.

But for now, peace.

Lord, you have invited us to give all our cares to you. In this world of anxiety
and worry, help me to hand over all my fears for your fire. Amen.

The name of the LORD is a strong tower;
the righteous run into it and are safe.
Proverbs 18:10 (NRSV)

THE NAME OF REFUGE

Holy Father, protect them by the power of your name, the name you gave me,
so that they may be one as we are one.
John 17:11 (NIV)

‿ِ‿

My name is stronger than rock, mightier than armies on high ground, sharper than the knife on your hip. Hold your head up! See me. I am your protection.

Do you fear? Come to me, and I will give you refuge. There is no better armor, no defender more vigilant. Perfect weakness will become perfect strength. I will speak to you my name. Even a whisper is enough.

I am still afraid.

Do not trust the man who says that steel is strongest or that blood will halt your enemy or that joy is the price of safety. Fear makes fools of many, and the best armed are often the most afraid.

Help me trust you, Lord, and not myself.

I will, by my name.

Of all the terrors in this world, the worst is this: forever asking who you are, but never hearing the answer.

‿ِ‿

Lord, your name is protection against all evil. You have given it
to your people freely and called us by it. Help me hear who I am,
and thus find rest and refuge in only you. Amen.

He does according to his will among the host of heaven
and among the inhabitants of the earth;
and none can stay his hand.

Daniel 4:35 (ESV)

NONE CAN STAY

This is the will of God, your sanctification.

1 Thessalonians 4:3 (NRSV)

How much I love you.
Never has there been a moment when you were outside my care.
Never a moment of forgetting.
Never once have I been faithless to you.

 It's true.

So I will promise you this, in my name, by the force of my
 unopposable will:
You will become holy, as I am.

 It's so hard, though.

Ah! But none can stay my hand,
and none of your rot can stay.
Let my joy triumph, cutting the darkness until all has fled
like shadows at the arrival of dawn.
I love you too much—
too much to leave you alone,
too much to leave in you any foolishness,
too much to let anything come between us.
Even your dearest sin.

*Lord, your will is perfect and no one can stop you from anything you
decide to do. Please help me surrender to your will, which is my sanctification.
Please help me embrace your plan, which is our perfect love. Amen.*

The meek shall inherit the land
and delight themselves in abundant peace.
Psalm 37:11 (ESV)

THE LEGACY OF PEACE

Blessed are the meek, for they will inherit the earth.
Matthew 5:5 (NRSV)

The earth will blossom in the coming day, when the kingdom invisible becomes the kingdom seen. Children and slaves will hold the thrones of the world. War will rust and be laid to sleep with the dead, and everyone will see the meek have always been the blessed ones.

May I be found worthy on that day, Father.

Let me worry about "someday" worthiness. Concern yourself with your "right-now" heart. Let your weapons forget why they were made and your wish for war languish. Let your strength be found in the peace you bring with you. Let the light of your eyes hold a promise of inheritance: to comfort the meek, to terrify the mighty, and to make the heart of your Father glad you are his legacy.

Lord, all peace is yours. Let me live as a citizen of your true kingdom today, despite the temptations of violence and conflict that surround me. Amen.

All these things my hand has made,
and so all these things are mine, says the LORD.
But this is the one to whom I will look,
to the humble and contrite in spirit, who trembles at my word.
Isaiah 66:2 (NRSV)

THE TREMBLING WORK

Continue to work out your salvation with fear and trembling, for it is
God who works in you to will and to act in order to fulfill his good purpose.
Philippians 2:12–13 (NIV)

You are my workmanship, a good and beautiful thing in whom I delight.
All that I make is mine, and so there is nothing that does not belong to
me. I wish to call you into the perfect love of eternity.

You are generous.

I have done all that was needed. But I still call you to join me in my work.
Create with me, build, encourage, love. Do. Be. Persevere in both. To
begin this work is no difficult thing, but to persist to the end, to overcome
all who dare challenge—that is a story worth telling angels, a fight cherubs
crane their wings to watch.

What must I do?

Fight to be simple of heart—to stand under the blood on the doorway,
sprinkled by the sopping sacrifice, wrapped in the white cloak. This is the
working of your salvation: to tremble upon the threshold—not at the one
who walks in night beyond the door, but at me, who stands behind the
ravening spirit, holding the lives of everyone and the fate of the host of
heaven, yearning beyond words for you to know and choose and bend
the knee and love what is most lovely in all the worlds. Longing for you
to tremble with Christ's dying, with Christ's life.

What must you do? Believe. And work. For all believing work is worship, and all true worship is my will.

Lord, you are the maker of all good things.
Help me work out the gift of life that you have given me. Amen.

Who is a God like you,
who pardons sin and forgives the transgression
of the remnant of his inheritance?
You do not stay angry forever
but delight to show mercy.

Micah 7:18 (NIV)

MERCY, MERCY

Blessed are the merciful, for they will receive mercy.

Matthew 5:7 (NRSV)

What do you hold in your heart against another?
Do you dream of vengeance and repayment upon the one who has
harmed you?
Has justice twisted itself in your chest so that you no longer think that
mercy is good?
Open your hand.

> *I can't.*
> *It's hard.*
> *Lord, it is so hard.*

Learn from me. I have been wronged by all.
And my mercy goes to each of you.

Let go.
Let go.
Let go.

Love.

Lord, you are the great Victim of every sin and the great Victor over
every brokenness. Show your victory over my own unforgiveness,
and help me release to you all bitterness I hold against others. Amen.

Create in me a pure heart, O God,
and renew a steadfast spirit within me.
Psalm 51:10 (NIV)

PURE

Blessed are the pure in heart, for they will see God.
Matthew 5:8 (NRSV)

⌣

When will you be pure? When will your own heart stop deceiving you?
When will you know the depth of your sickness and the double-depth of
my healing?

> *silence*

[silence]

> *silence*

[silence]

> *silence*

[silence]

> *silence*

You will know all this and more when you see me as I am, not as you
want me to be.

⌣

Lord, you are perfect in holiness. Make me pure—all of me—
that I may see you as you are, in your power and goodness. Amen.

*The kingdom of heaven is like treasure hidden in a field, which someone found
and hid; then in his joy he goes and sells all that he has and buys that field.*

Matthew 13:44 (NRSV)

THE HOLY CON

*I have suffered the loss of all things . . . that I may gain Christ and
be found in him. . . . I want to know Christ and the power of his resurrection
and the sharing of his sufferings by becoming like him in his death,
if somehow I may attain the resurrection from the dead.*

Philippians 3:8–11 (NRSV)

All your life, you have toiled to gather what others told you was valuable.
It is a burden, hard to bear.

*The heavier the load, the more precious the cargo.
What weighs much, pays much, right?*

Run to the Man ahead on the road. Tell him that saying. He will chuckle
and take your arm, and while you walk, he'll tell you that the burden of
heaven is so light you can leap with it and that anyone who says differently is ripping you off.

"Give me your baggage," he'll say, "and when I'm king, you'll have a
kingdom in return."

You will think it a scam. He wants all you have worked for, all you have
bled for, all that seems worth its weight in life. You will think he's conning you, until you see his eyes, and understand, and happily swap your
whole life for the promise that glitters in them.

At that moment, you will have traded nothing worth keeping for more
than you ever dared to desire.

*Lord, your burden is easy, your yoke is light, and your kingdom is true treasure.
Help me value you above all else, giving all up for your sake. Amen.*

Restore us to yourself, O LORD, that we may be restored.
Lamentations 5:21 (NRSV)

THE RESTORING TIME

Repent . . . and turn back, that your sins may be blotted out, that times of refreshing
may come from the presence of the Lord, and that he may send the Christ
appointed for you, Jesus, whom heaven must receive until the time for restoring.
Acts 3:19–21 (ESV)

ــِ))

Lord, only you can make things right.
Help me.

Take heart, my child.
There is time for turning,
time for calling,
time for seeking,
time for asking,
time for knocking
and for opening,
time for sowing,
time for watering,
time for gathering,
time for eating,
time for waiting,
time for rejoicing,
time for mourning,
time for returning.
A time for restoring all things.

All times are one time,
and they are called "today."
It is shorter than you think,
and longer than you know.

Take heart.

ــِ))

Father, you have promised to restore all things in Jesus. May the time of full
restoration come quickly. While your people wait, restore us fully to yourself,
that we may lead holy lives in love with you. Amen.

You yourselves like living stones
are being built up as a spiritual house.
1 Peter 2:5 (ESV)

A LIVING STONE

For every house is built by someone,
but the builder of all things is God.
Hebrews 3:4 (ESV)

⁓

You are built with all the others—stones upon stones—held up by the Cornerstone, a rock that trips the world.

You are the house, the palace, the temple of God. You are the walls of the sanctuary, facing the desert on your outside and the holiest of holies within.

No stone in the wall knows its own importance, its own beauty, its own strength. Of no stone in my walls can it be said, "This one does not matter," nor can any be removed without loss, without weakening the whole.

You matter, little stone.

Really?

More than you know. You hold up others, just as others hold up you. Do not fall away, lest many crumble around you. You are laid with care and looked on with love. You are beautiful in strength, patterned according to your builder's own wish. My wish.

If you can believe it, this is the truth Abraham began to see: no grain of sand may be swept from the shore lightly, and no star dies without darkening the whole sky.

⁓

Lord, you have formed your people into a unity of diversity.
Please help me see and appreciate the role of every one of your
children in the family of God, and value my own life and role.
Let me be constant and strong. Amen.

Mortals cannot abide in their pomp;
they are like the animals that perish.

Psalm 49:12 (NRSV)

AS WITHIN, SO WITHOUT

The kingdom has departed from you! You shall be driven away from human society,
and your dwelling shall be with the animals of the field. You shall be made
to eat grass like oxen, and seven times shall pass over you, until you have
learned that the Most High has sovereignty over the kingdom of mortals.

Daniel 4:31–32 (NRSV)

It was a lovely morning in Babylon when Nebuchadnezzar rose from a scented bed he had cruelly strewn with concubines. The king strode upstairs to observe the crystal city. How it gleamed under the sun, the roofs and terraced gardens stretching in might and richness! Thinking himself the lord of something, the man stroked his braided beard and won seven years' fate with a single word: "Mine."

The Watchers waited at my command. With a word they laid him low. My verdict was not unjust, nor was it unthoughtful—I merely allowed his face and his posture to take the shape of his soul. He became the beast he already was.

It was just!

Indeed.

But what if I led you to such justice? If my decree bent your body to match your heart, what would you become? What if I made your inner life become your outer life, for anyone to see?

silence

How ought I to lead you? How are you to know the goodness of the one who teaches the world? When will you realize that all my lordship is love and that a humble beast is more like God than anyone's pride?

King of all, you are just and wise. I pray that I might be teachable and humble, wel-coming your rule in my life. Please let me honor you and give you all praise. Amen.

Father of orphans and protector of widows is God in his holy habitation.
God gives the desolate a home to live in; he leads out the prisoners to prosperity.
Psalm 68:5–6 (NRSV)

THE FULLNESS OF THE DESOLATE

You are being rooted and grounded in love. I pray that you may
have the power to comprehend, with all the saints, what is the breadth
and length and height and depth, and to know the love of Christ that
surpasses knowledge, so that you may be filled with all the fullness of God.
Ephesians 3:17–19 (NRSV)

There was never a moment when you were not loved. From your beginning, I counted you as my own, with all compassion, all gentleness, all steadfastness. Also with all rigor, with all strength, and with the love of discipline—for a Father teaches his children well if he loves them. And I love you.

There are two pillars that hold up the beauty of our way: kindness and strength. Both are good. Neither is easy.

Why do you ask so much of your children?
You make us struggle to draw near you.

That answer cannot be put into thought. It is only a name—and you already know it.

Jesus?

Yes. Run to me, trusting that I am the strength of the weak, that I am a rewarder of those who seek.

The earth cannot contain the love I have for you, and so it spills forever
upward, as broad as beauty,
as long as understanding, as high and deep as wisdom. It is a crown of
absolute compassion,
beyond all knowing, and, from atop the head of the bride, it fills all eternity.

Lord, you call all weak and humble things to yourself. May I know
the fullness of your love and goodness in the midst of my own shortcomings
and cling to you today, in the hope of perfect love. Amen.

I will ask the Father, and he will give you another Advocate,
to be with you forever. This is the Spirit of truth, whom the world
cannot receive, because it neither sees him nor knows him.
John 14:16–17 (NRSV)

TO CRY

You did not receive a spirit of slavery to fall back into fear, but you have
received a spirit of adoption. When we cry, "Abba! Father!" it is that very
Spirit bearing witness with our spirit that we are children of God.
Romans 8:15–16 (NRSV)

One of these days you will cry to me in a new way, the full meaning of "Father" behind your prayer. In crying that name, you will know the depth of faith, the right of a child to be heard. You will know expectation and provision; you will know joy.

No one else can fill a heart like I do. No one can be so whole in love. No one can be so strong in help, so patient in waiting, so joyful in every turning of your life. No one else can call you into life.

What is it you need today? Are you overwhelmed and burdened? Are you haunted by voices you do not want to hear, by shadows of the past, or taunts of the future? Does peace seem to escape you? Do you fear the darkness? Fear the morning?

Cry to me! There is nothing too small and nothing too great. Never yet have I heard that voice and remained silent.

Father!

Father, you know my heart, the requests that I long to bring in full
faith before you. Let my belief in your provision be complete,
looking in trust to you, and waiting for your will. Amen.

As a father has compassion for his children,
so the LORD has compassion for those who fear him.
For he knows how we were made;
he remembers that we are dust.
Psalm 103:13–14 (NRSV)

A CONSOLATION

Blessed be the God and Father of our Lord Jesus Christ, the Father of mercies
and the God of all consolation, who consoles us in all our affliction.
2 Corinthians 1:3–4 (NRSV)

What pains you?

You know.

I would like you to tell me.

Why?

Because I love you.

What pains you?

It all pains me.
The work, the hurt, the confusion, the weariness of living.

I have felt those things, and today I feel your pain in them as only a parent can. So great is my love for you—so keen my every emotion, so deep my compassion, so intricate my affection—that if you experienced it all at once it would split you, like new wine bursts a wineskin. No child easily understands the comforting of their parent.

Be patient; know you are my own. Know that the Father of Lights grips you and that every spring bud bears the promise of your far future. The promise to be perfectly held, fearless and only yourself. The promise that you will gather perfect fruit forever under a riper sun than this. I have loved much, and I do not lose my own, for I unleash my fierce and fighting joy against every darkness.

Lord, you are perfect in love, and you are the abundant comforter
of your people. You know all my pain and worry.
Help me trust you and turn to you for consolation. Amen.

God chose what is foolish in the world to shame the wise;
God chose what is weak in the world to shame the strong; God chose what
is low and despised in the world, things that are not, to reduce to nothing
things that are, so that no one might boast in the presence of God.
1 Corinthians 1:27–29 (NRSV)

ON THE DEATH OF BOASTING

Who dares despise the day of small things?
Zechariah 4:10 (NIV)

෴

My sight is perfect, seven eyes surveying the earth.
To me all hearts are open, from me no secrets are hid.
I have seen all who think themselves great and all who know themselves
to be nothing.
I have disturbed the proud, and strengthened the humble.

> *Praise you. But I am afraid.*

Christ will be your shield.
In the bones of all I have placed a summons that cannot be denied:

YOU ARE CALLED TO RECKON FULL ACCOUNTS BEFORE THE LORD OF LIFE,
FOR ALL THAT YOU ARE AND ALL THAT YOU HAVE DONE,
WHETHER ON THAT DAY YOU BE FOUND DEAD OR ALIVE.

Every soul will be presented before the seat of the All-knowing.
You will be among them, and, oh, what things you will see!

Up will I raise the bowed heads!
Away will I wipe the tears of pain and contrition!
Strong will I make the feeble knees! Light will I make the heart that is heavy!
And I will bend the back of the proud
and splay wicked fingers so they can harm no more.
With wisdom I will slice open the cruel fool from thigh to neck.
With the Cornerstone I will crush the head of the proud.
The earth will be forever free, and its joy will be complete.

෴

Father, you judge justly. Help me humble myself before you,
knowing that you are pleased by humility and simplicity. Amen.

THE WALKING CITY

*Prepare your minds for action; discipline yourselves; set all your hope
on the grace that Jesus Christ will bring you when he is revealed.*

1 Peter 1:13 (NRSV)

Look, if you are vigilant, and see two paths.
You are presented with both every day.
The path of life and the path of death.
The path of wisdom and the path of foolishness.
The path of the Son and the path of the Tempter.
The narrow and the wide,
the true and the bent,
the finding and the losing.
The path home. The path away.

How do I know which is which?

Sight is a gift, but it must be opened.
To any who asks I will grant wisdom, but it is up to the receiver to be
disciplined and use it.
Every pilgrim is a city unto themselves. They may be vigilant in life and
insight, or lax.
Oh, walking city, learn to defend yourself. Keep guards upon your walls.
Keep your gates open, but ensure they are strong. Welcome all, but only
let my Spirit dwell.

Keep to the trail of Christ.
Every step will seem somehow both harder and easier than the one you
took before.
This is how you'll know you are headed home.

*Lord, in Christ you have shown us a model of perfect self-control and discipline.
Help me learn to do even what is hard for me to do, so that I may walk wisely,
imitating Jesus, who did what he saw you doing. Amen.*

THE TURNING

I never forgot you.

Mornings and evenings, I heard silences in the halls of our house where your steps and laughter should have been, and I ached. I listened for you along the paths of our garden, under the fig tree, and among family at the table, where every laugh had a ring of sadness to it and a plate always seemed to be missing.

You were never as far from me as you thought.

At night in my room I saw your face in my mind. Because you were not close enough to bless with my hands, I blessed you in my heart. I willed that the world that had lured you away should weather and wither you until you turned, ready to be held. "Come," I whispered into the night.

And here you are.

I am so sorry, Father. I–

We should not be talking. We should be eating! Everyone will be so excited to see you. Come on, I'll race you back to the door.

Lord, you are a kind and loving father to all your children, whether they are
close or far from you. Thank you for welcoming me always to your family. Help
me turn fully to you and give you all my affection and a child's pure love. Amen.

Peter began to speak to them: "I truly understand that God shows no partiality, but in every nation anyone who fears him and does what is right is acceptable to him. You know the message he sent to the people of Israel, preaching peace by Jesus Christ—he is Lord of all."
Acts 10:34–36 (NRSV)

REGARDING SUPPERTIME

Here I am! I stand at the door and knock. If anyone hears my voice and opens the door, I will come in and eat with that person, and they with me.
Revelation 3:20 (NIV)

⟞

Seriously, Father—anyone?

Anyone.

Surely not—

Anyone.

But the—

Anyone.

I don't know if you understand—

I know exactly who you hope I'll leave out, who you think is not worthy of eating and drinking with me, whether at their table or at mine.

Listen. If you keep going on like this, I'm going to seat you right next to them at supper and ask you to pour their wine and pass them the bread.

If you don't like unworthy company, you'll hate heaven.

⟞

*Father, you show favor to all, regardless of our worthiness before you.
I repent of thinking that some people should not be brought into your community, and pray that you would give me your gracious nature. Amen.*

As for mortals, their days are like grass; they flourish like a flower of the field;
for the wind passes over it, and it is gone, and its place knows it no more.
Psalm 103:15–16 (NRSV)

LIKE GRASS

Surely the people are grass. The grass withers, the flower fades;
but the word of our God will stand forever.
Isaiah 40:7–8 (NRSV)

ﮮ

Every green sprout thinks it is immortal as it pushes up from the wet earth. How I love the new growth, the innocent blades of spring! The days that lengthen toward summer speak love to the grass. The rain waters it, and the breeze prickles dew on the leaves. But how soon the mowers come. How soon the grazing beasts crush the stalks to cud. How soon little dancers trample the lawns. All grass dies, and so too the flowers among it. By the first frosts, it has passed long away, brown into decay.

I am like that.

Yes, you are. Every child thinks they are immortal as they push into the light of life. And how I love them for it!

How I loved you, watching your eyes first squint against the sun. You will pass from this earth in your season, but how loved you have been every day of your life upon it. How you will continue to be loved in the life that is coming.

But I am afraid. Nothing lasts!

You know that I last, perfect in life and love. You know that my word is eternal, incorruptible. You know that Christ has set your life in eternal safety. Your body will fade and await the resurrection, but your life is secure already in a place beyond time, beyond death, beyond decay. You are treasured, grass-child. I rooted you where the sickle cannot reach. And it is there that I will show you how richly your kind can flower—forever.

ﮮ

Lord, you are eternal and unchanging. I am frail and mortal, conscious of
my own weakness. Help me begin to live your eternal life in this world,
leading many others to know the hope of life in Christ Jesus. Amen.

The LORD bless you and keep you;
the LORD make his face shine on you and be gracious to you;
the LORD turn his face toward you and give you peace.
Numbers 6:24–26 (NIV)

TO BLESS THE BRANCHES

He will make your righteous reward shine like the dawn,
your vindication like the noonday sun.
Psalm 37:6 (NIV)

ﻭ

You who hear this, whether with much faith or little:
be blessed.

Let the sun guard and warm you, the Son give you strength.
Let all fear flee,
until confusion and wickedness have no place near you.

May peace bloom for you into a blossom that cannot fade,
may justice be found by you and in you.
May the blood of Christ be water and wine,
his flesh be bread, his Spirit oil in the fields of the sowers and reapers.

I receive it all.

Now friend, come up higher!
Climb the tree of life–
the branches are wide and strong enough for all.
Reach from beauty,
stretching to understanding,
pulling up on wisdom,
until you come into sight of the place where I hang,
beyond words, above the healing leaves, high above the kingdom.
There you will know me, just as you are known,
as the crown and light of the listening day.

ﻭ

Holy Father, king of all worlds, you have called me to follow
Jesus and approach your perfect presence. Let all of life lead me to you
through the Holy Spirit, and may I know you in your fullness,
through all this life and in the life that is to come. Amen.

Holy, holy, holy,
is the Lord God Almighty,
who was, and who is,
and who is to come.

ACKNOWLEDGMENTS

This book could never have happened without the ideas, encouragement, wisdom, and faith of Don Jacobson. His idea first set this project rolling, and to him and his wife, Brenda, I owe so much. They walk the path of the righteous, and it is bright indeed. I am inspired by their faith and their zeal.

Laurel Boruck was instrumental in "getting" this project from the beginning. Every aspect of the book is better for her brilliant creative contributions.

Thanks, too, for the input of Tawny Johnson and Marty Raz; they were intimately involved in the production of the manuscript.

Melissa Binder brought a sharp editor's eye to this book—with deep belief, enthusiasm, grammatical stickling, and good questions. The book is much clearer and more beautiful because of her.

Connie Gabbert not only created the cover designs for this series, she made true art with them. I stand in humble awe of her work.

My beloved wife, Emily, contributed honest and constant encouragement and deep insights. This book exists because of her support, open mind, and rich faith.

The Lord has never once failed to meet me when I asked it of him. Though his words were often convicting, they brought life with them, a life which I hope may be found on every page of this book. To him be all glory, from the dust of the kingdom to the perfect crown.

Listening to his voice for eternity will indeed be heaven.

ABOUT THE AUTHOR

Paul J. Pastor is a writer living in Oregon's Columbia River Gorge. His writing on Christian spirituality has won numerous awards and critical recognition for its beauty, insight, and biblical depth. With an MA in Biblical and Theological Studies from Western Seminary, Paul brings his passionate style and unique insights to life as a frequent speaker at churches and universities.

Paul and his wife Emily serve as deacons of spiritual formation at Theophilus Church in Portland, Oregon. They have three children, a brook running through their garden, and a view of the best sunrise in the world.

If you'd like to write a note to Paul, you may send it to PO Box 36, Bridal Veil, OR 97010

Also by Paul J. Pastor

ⓩ | ZEALbooks

Portland, Oregon

Zeal Books is a new publisher dedicated to world-changing ideas. We're focused and founded on love—love for our authors and love for their books. And love makes you zealous. Zeal's commitment to its authors, readers, and accounts is to only publish books we're zealous for—books the world needs.

Visit us online for news, resources, and more at zealbooks.com, or find us on social media:

🐦 @ZealBks

📷 @ZealBks

f facebook.com/zealbks

Other Zeal Titles